WRITING AGAINST THE SILENCE:
JOY KOGAWA'S *OBASAN*

Canadian Fiction Studies

Additional volumes in preparation

•

Writing Against the Silence:
JOY KOGAWA'S

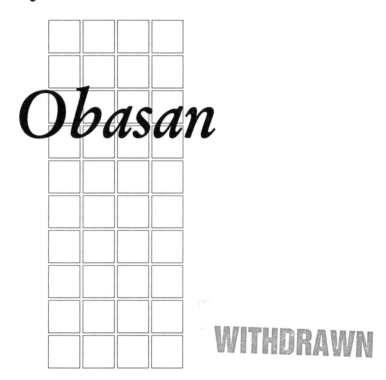

Obasan

WITHDRAWN

Arnold Davidson

E C W   P R E S S

CANADIAN CATALOGUING IN PUBLICATION DATA

Davidson, Arnold E., 1936–
Writing against the silence : Joy Kogawa's Obasan

(Canadian fiction studies ; 30)
Includes bibliographical references and index.
ISBN 1-55022-179-5
I. Kogawa, Joy. Obasan.
I. Title. II. Series.

PS8521.0440234 1993   C813'.54   C94-930011-X
PR9199.3.K630234 1993

This book has been published with the assistance of the
Ministry of Culture, Recreation and Tourism of the Province
of Ontario, through funds provided by the Ontario
Publishing Centre, and with the assistance of grants from
The Canada Council, the Ontario Arts Council, and the
Government of Canada through the Department of
Communications, and the Canadian Studies and Special Projects
Directorate of the Department of the Secretary of State of Canada.

The cover features a reproduction of the dust-wrapper
from the first edition of Obasan, courtesy of the
Thomas Fisher Rare Book Library, University of Toronto.
Frontispiece photograph by John Flanders,
reproduced with his permission.
Design and imaging by ECW Type & Art, Oakville, Ontario.
Printed and bound by Kromar Printing, Winnipeg, Manitoba.

Distributed by General Distribution Services,
30 Lesmill Road, Don Mills, Ontario M3B 2T6.

Published by ECW PRESS,
1980 Queen Street East,
Toronto, Ontario M4L 1J2.

Table of Contents

A Note on the Author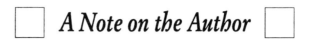

Arnold E. Davidson grew up in southern Alberta, not far from the town of Coaldale where Joy Kogawa's family was sent. After graduating from high school, he entered the University of Chicago and received a BA in anthropology and an MA in English. He then taught English for a number of years at Elmhurst College in Illinois before attending the State University of New York at Binghamton, where he wrote his PhD thesis on Joseph Conrad under the direction of Robert Kroetsch. That fortuitous experience fostered a renewed interest in Canadian authors, and he began to publish numerous essays on contemporary Canadian novelists and poets. In 1983 he left Elmhurst College to be a professor of English at Michigan State University and to teach in that institution's Canadian Studies Centre. In 1989 he accepted the position of research professor of Canadian Studies at Duke University. He has also taught twice, each time for a year, in Japan as a visiting professor of Canadian and British literature, and he has given papers on Canadian literature in Canada, the United States, France, Spain, and Japan. In addition to writing books on Joseph Conrad, Jean Rhys, Mordecai Richler, and the Canadian Western, he has coedited (with Cathy N. Davidson) *The Art of Margaret Atwood*, has edited for the Modern Language Association *Studies on Canadian Literature: Introductory and Critical Essays*, and has published some 75 articles, most of them on Canadian writing.

REFERENCES AND ACKNOWLEDGEMENTS

All page references to *Obasan* are given parenthetically in the text and are to the widely available paperback Penguin edition first published in 1983. This edition, incidentally, uses the same pagination as the original 1981 Lester and Orpen Dennys edition.

I would like to thank, first, my two research assistants, Glenn Willmott and Julia Dryer, for helping with this project, and, second, Jennifer Huntley for being, again, an exemplary typist.

This book is dedicated to Cathy, my partner in Japan, as elsewhere, and to my Japanese friends, colleagues, and students who have taught me much about *Obasan*.

Writing Against the Silence:
Joy Kogawa's *Obasan*

Chronology

1877–1928 Japanese immigrants (the *Issei*, or first generation away from Japan) arrive in Canada and settle mostly in or near Vancouver and Victoria and in smaller towns and villages along the Pacific Coast.

1895   All Japanese settlers and their descendants are denied the vote in British Columbia. The Privy Council later upholds this law whereby naturalized or Canadian-born British subjects can be barred from voting in provincial elections and, in effect, denied other privileges and positions granted only to duly registered voters.

1907   Anti-Asian riots take place in Vancouver. Japan, at Canada's insistence, agrees to limit male immigrants to 400 per year. Before this agreement, most Japanese immigrants were men; afterwards, most are women coming to join their husbands.

1928   Canada establishes a quota of 150 Japanese immigrants per year, a quota that, in subsequent years, it seldom allows to be filled.

1935   Joy Nozomi Nakayama is born on 6 June in Vancouver, where her father is a minister and her mother a kindergarten teacher.

1940   All Japanese immigration is halted.

1941   Immediately after the 7 December Japanese attack on Pearl Harbor, Canada declares war on Japan.

1942   Various orders in council made under the War Measures Act require that all those of Japanese ancestry living within 100 miles of the Pacific Coast be removed from this "protected area." Some 21,000 people, three quarters

9

of whom are Canadian citizens, are sent into internal exile, mostly to work camps and detention camps in the interior of British Columbia. They are allowed to retain only those personal goods that they can carry with them. The rest of their property is confiscated and sold at fire-sale prices, with much of the proceeds going to pay for the costs of this massive relocation.

1942–45   The Nakayama family is evacuated to Slocan in the interior of British Columbia, where they remain for the duration of the war.

1945   After the defeat of Japan, Japanese Canadians are required to choose between "repatriation" to that war-ravaged country or another dispersal east of the Rockies. Most pick the second alternative. The Nakayama family is moved to Coaldale, Alberta.

1946   A government proposal to deport to Japan 10,000 Japanese Canadians elicits a massive public protest and is dropped.

1949   Japanese Canadians are finally allowed to return to the Pacific Coast, and are given the vote.

1953   Joy Nakayama attends the University of Alberta in Edmonton for a one-year teacher-training program.

1954   Returns to Coaldale to teach elementary school.

1955   Moves to Toronto to attend the Royal Conservatory of Music.

1956   Moves to Vancouver.

1957   Marries David Kogawa. The family lives in Vancouver, Grand Forks, Moose Jaw, and Saskatoon before moving to Ottawa. Gordon Kogawa is born on 17 November.

1959   Deidre Kogawa is born on 30 October.

1967   *The Splintered Moon* (poetry) is published. Canada rescinds the prohibition on immigration from Japan.

1968   Divorces David Kogawa.

1969   Travels to and in Japan.

1974   *A Choice of Dreams* (poetry) is published.

1974–76   Works as a staff writer in the office of the prime minister.

1977	*Jericho Road* (poetry) is published.
1978	Becomes writer in residence at the University of Ottawa.
1979	Moves to Toronto, where she still resides.
1981	*Obasan* is published and wins the *Books in Canada* First Novel Award.
1982	*Obasan* wins the Canadian Authors' Association Book of the Year Award.
1983	Japanese Canadians petition, through the National Association of Japanese Canadians, for an official apology and compensation, but the Liberal government of Pierre Trudeau is opposed to offering either. Brian Mulroney, as the opposition leader, criticizes this decision and subsequently makes a campaign promise to negotiate a settlement, but after his 1984 election various federal negotiators in his Conservative government find reasons for not agreeing to pay any individual compensation.
1984	Again visits Japan.
1985	*Woman in the Woods* (poetry) is published.
1986	*Naomi's Road* (a juvenile-fiction version of *Obasan*) is published.
1988	Prime Minister Brian Mulroney formally apologizes for the "past injustices" Japanese Canadians had been forced to endure, and the Canadian government agrees to pay $21,000 each to the approximately 12,000 surviving Japanese Canadians who were dispossessed and interned during World War II. (Earlier in the year the United States government had agreed to pay $20,000 to each survivor of the American internment.)
1992	*Itsuka* (a novel) is published.

The Importance of the Work

Obasan is one of the most important Canadian books to appear in recent decades and is so, I would maintain, for three basic reasons. The novel is socially significant because it tells us something about ourselves as a society that we long preferred not to hear. The novel is artistically significant because it tells us unpalatable truths with consummate art. The novel is culturally significant because, thanks to the very art with which it addresses large social questions, it claims a special place for the ethnic writer in the ostensibly bicultural context of Canada and thereby encourages us to rethink our paradigms for Canadian culture and literature. Such summary listing, however, hardly does justice to the importance of *Obasan*, so, in the paragraphs to follow, I shall briefly expand upon all three considerations, starting with the first.

"Canadians," a major Canadian historian has observed,

like to describe their country as "a peaceable kingdom," little touched by the effects of war. They also cherish the notion that immigrants to Canada flourish in a tolerant "multicultural mosaic," rather than struggle against the assimilative "melting pot" of the United States. (3)

But "both of these myths of . . . national self-image" (3), as John Herd Thompson insists, were contradicted by Canada's treatment of ethnic "enemy" minorities during both world wars, and they were particularly contradicted by the treatment of Japanese Canadians during and after World War II.

Powerfully portraying that mistreatment and its racist rationale, *Obasan* effectively counters the country's preferred image of itself and attests that the national metaphor of the mosaic is sometimes honoured more in the breach than in the observance. Indeed, the facts of the case of Japanese Canadians, as set forth in *Obasan*, are so stark and devastating that we read the novel "with a mixture of curiosity, shame, and horror [that] must be what a German feels, reminded of Nazi atrocities" (Moss 201). The Nazis, of course, were more brutally criminal, but the Canadians were more conveniently hypocritical, so the equation between the two that John Moss draws — and that is drawn in the novel — is not untenable. What is untenable is the racism implicit in the decision to dispossess and exile all Pacific Coast residents of Japanese ancestry, whether Canadian citizens or not, on the unsubstantiated suspicion that their allegiance would be to Japan once Canada had declared war on that country. Because it prompts the painful awareness that this racism was carried to an almost Nazi excess, *Obasan* is, for Canada, a kind of hall of shame.

Every society, I suggest when I teach the novel, should have some such rogue's gallery where its worst misdeeds could be publicly commemorated instead of being swept under the carpet of a conveniently forgetful history. There would then be some belated justice for both victims and perpetrators. In this sense, "it's unfortunate that Mackenzie King isn't [still alive and] able to read" *Obasan* (John Richardson, qtd. in "Ode" 5). In this sense, too, a hall of shame could have a definite salutary effect. Perhaps Mackenzie King, for example, might have been a less sleazy and hypocritical prime minister had he suspected that he would be remembered for those qualities.

But just as *Obasan* places us, as Canadians, in a hall of shame, it also shows us at least partly how to get out. The indictment of the book is, by extension, a call to action, a demand that something be done to oppose, to set right, as much as possible, the wrongs exposed. The injustice portrayed in the novel was still very much with us when *Obasan* was published in 1981. It was, in fact, still not even officially acknowledged, and thus the novel immediately provided a powerful literary lever for Japanese Canadians attempting to gain an official apology and some redress. As Kogawa's entry in the 1991 *Canada's Who's Who* attests, her work was "instrumental in influencing the Candn. Govt.'s 1988 settlement with Japanese-Canadians for their loss of liberty and property in Canada during World War II" ("Kogawa, Joy" 552). Moreover, when the government finally passed the measure whereby it apologized and awarded each survivor restitution of $21,000, "parts of *Obasan* were read in the Canadian

House of Commons . . ." as a fitting tribute to the novel's role in achieving this end (Goellnicht 306n28). Desirable as that end was, however, it hardly concluded the matter. Are not prejudice and hate, Naomi several times asks in the novel, always with us? Once in a hall of shame, the only way out, the novel makes clear, is to be perpetually engaged in dismantling that edifice and everything for which it stands.

In telling us who we are and what we need to do about it, *Obasan*, as John Moss notes, is "documentary" and "didactic" (201). Yet it is so in crucial ways that negate the usually negative connotations of those adjectives as applied to novels. Moreover, and as Moss insists, this text "is not an artifact of history but a vision of the truth" (201). The work is important because it has the artistic integrity, the fictional craft, and the verbal facility required to communicate that vision. "Write the vision and make it plain" (31). This biblical exhortation is passed on in the novel from one character to another, but mostly it is partially heeded only by the author herself, who well knows the danger of too much plainness. To be more than a political tract on the mistreatment of Japanese Canadians, the book has to engage the reader, and is, accordingly, written in a style that is almost Japanese — imagistic, indirect, allusive. It is subtly structured through recurrent scenes, actions, images, dreams, and verbal echoes that also serve to involve the reader, to entangle him or her in the web (one of the recurring metaphors) of the writer's art. This web is so finely spun that *Obasan* must be deemed a major work of art. As such, it demands and repays a careful analytic reading, and only through such a reading can the full extent of Kogawa's artistic accomplishment begin to be appreciated.

The art of *Obasan* will be considered in much greater detail in the major section of this study, "Reading of the Text," so to conclude this overview assessment of the work's importance I would here note how it has helped to position, in a particularly Canadian context (remember the mosaic), the ethnic novel. Most obviously, by brilliantly conjoining both sides of Japanese-Canadian experience, *Obasan* demonstrates a way to escape from what E.D. Blodgett has identified as the bind of binarism. This assumption that two cultures, two languages, and two literatures divide one country leaves little room for anything else, and necessarily discourages ethnic writers. *Obasan*, however, conclusively attests that Japanese Canadians — as well as Canadians of any stripe, break, or hyphen whatever — have a place in the country and a place in the country's literature.

The ethnic writer, by claiming her or his place, also raises crucial questions about what we might call representational rights. Such questions are foregrounded in *Obasan* when Japanese-Canadian characters view with utter disbelief and dismay the way the surrounding white society views them. Thus Naomi reads a newspaper clipping about the 1945 sugar-beet harvest that is accompanied by a photo of Japanese farm workers captioned "Grinning and Happy" (193). The printed "facts" about the record harvest and the "evacuee" workers are not, however, her facts: "The fact is I never got used to it and I cannot, I cannot bear the memory. There are some nightmares from which there is no waking" (194). Naomi's rendering of what is, after all, her nightmare is rather more persuasive than the "grinning and happy" photo that needs only watermelons to be the complete cliché of "happy workers" down on the farm not at all minding their enforced servitude. In short, the captioned photo is hardly a portrait of "them" but a portrait of "us" as revealed by how we see what we do to others. *Obasan* is important for thus demonstrating the colonial and postcolonial implications of representation itself.[1] Any real multiculturalism must allow others to provide their own stories, to represent themselves instead of acceding to representations conveniently advanced by more dominant groups and voices with their own interests to serve.

The novel does not, however, resolve the vexing current question of just who has rights to what group's stories.[2] But it does suggest from what quarters the most telling versions are likely to come, and has therefore helped to lay the groundwork for the recent flourishing of ethnic fiction in Canada as seen, for example, in Nino Ricci's *Lives of the Saints* winning a 1990 Governor-General's award, and Rohinton Mistry's *Such a Long Journey* winning a 1991 one.

Critical Reception

Obasan has been praised from the first, both within Canada and beyond, as a "tour de force" depiction of the fate of Japanese Canadians during World War II and after (Milton 17; Wayne 34). Indeed, the early reviews emphasize how forcefully the novel confronts the racism underlying a "national exercise in pernicious lunacy" whereby Japanese Canadians were deprived of their rights, property, and twice sent into socially devastating internal exile (Milton 8), but they also note how the author's subtle artistic control transforms the tragic history into transcendent narrative. Comparing Joy Kogawa to Toni Morrison and Maxine Hong Kingston, Kathryn Kilgore, for instance, particularly admires the "double-edged vision" that allows *Obasan* "to tell not only the experience of an individual, and through that the experience of a minority culture, but also the delusions of the dominant culture," and to tell, moreover, these different but related Chinese-box stories so powerfully that "the repetition of accurately selected, pointed details . . . work[s] the pattern of the story right through your skin" (45).

The imagery of Kilgore's encomium (the artistry of the book engraving its "sentence" even into the reader's flesh) hints at what Milton more explicitly formulates, the "anguished tension between [Kogawa's] graceful prose and the essential power and despair of her story" (8). Other reviewers also make much the same point. For Joyce Wayne, the "[b]eautifully structured" novel conjoins "documentary precision with a heightened emotional state pulled taut, almost to the breaking point" (34). William French asserts: "Its power comes from the beauty of the writing, the stark imagery and vivid symbolism, and from the calm recitation of events that destroyed families, a culture and a way of life" (15). Beyond the subject/

art dichotomy (which is to be expected, after all, in reviews), such comments suggest another important aspect of the novel — that it breaks down this dichotomy by pushing art to the breaking point to portray characters pushed to the breaking point, to force articulate story out of silenced history. All in all, *Obasan* was well served by its first reviewers.

There are, however, a few ominous notes in the early notice the novel received. One reviewer, for example, describes a Japanese-Canadian character as "clacking loudly and demanding redress" (Collins 54), as if this reaction were somehow less seemly than the actions that caused it. Similarly, in a joint review of *Obasan* and Ann Gomer Sunahara's *The Politics of Racism* (a good assessment of the historical and social background of the novel), Hilda L. Thomas complains of "the reticent, even apologetic tone of Sunahara's [Japanese Canadian] informants," and then goes on to observe that "when even the victims of injustice appear unmoved by their experience, it is hard for a reader unfamiliar with the event to grasp the full extent of the injury inflicted under the guise of necessity" (103). We have here more than the "guise of necessity" masking and muting "the full extent of the injury." Is the beating of others into silence somehow excused by the consideration that those others did not — and do not — effectively complain? Furthermore, what is a victim to do? Clack indecorously (and, as *Obasan* attests, mostly ineffectually) or silently endure in complicit dignity? Even to pose the question is to miss a basic point in the novel. Kogawa told one reviewer that "she called her book *Obasan* because Obasan 'is totally silent.' She is a carefully drawn portrait of the oppressed. 'If we never really see Obasan, she will always be oppressed. How [Kogawa asks] does society stop oppressing those who never speak up?'" (Wayne 34).

A certain discomfort with the subject and implications of *Obasan* is elsewhere evident as well. The *Books in Canada* article announcing that it had won that publication's award for first novels was atrociously titled "Ode to Joy," a bad pun on the author's name made even more dubious by the half-niggling tone of the announcement itself. According to *Quill and Quire*, "*Obasan* emerged not as the clear choice of the judges, but as the contender that escaped least bruised by their critical jabs" ("Joy Kogawa" 26). One judge, for example, "was certainly outraged by [the events portrayed in]

Obasan," but found it "too . . . documentary," and passed it over for "the only" work "that made me laugh ("Ode" 4). Another preferred George Jonas's *Final Decree*, which did come close to winning. But in this account of an immigrant's misadventures in Canada, the main impediment to happiness and success is "fuzzy feminism" ("Ode" 5), a much safer object of the ethnic writer's ire than the nation's "meanness of spirit" portrayed in Kogawa's "devastating statement about this country" (Martin 1).

As Donald Goellnicht observes, "[a]ll the reviews I have seen" of *Obasan* preponderantly "praise [both] Kogawa's poetic style" and the way that the novel sets the historical "record straight" by "resurrecting a [hitherto suppressed] piece of Canada's heritage" (287), its mistreatment of West Coast Japanese Canadians. Not surprisingly, a number of subsequent critics such as Carol Fairbanks, Mason Harris, Coral Ann Howells, Marilyn Russell Rose, B.A. St. Andrews, and Gary Willis have followed these already well-worn paths, but Goellnicht does not intend to do so himself. Because history, he insists, is not "unproblematic" and cannot be recovered through "transparently referential" language, "a major point of Kogawa's fiction" is the way that it "problematizes the very act of reconstructing history" (287). Although Goellnicht then proceeds to present quite unproblematically much of the history in question — "summariz[ing, for example,] some of the recent, and long overdue, historical accounts of the internment, evacuation, and dispersal of Japanese Canadians during and after the Second World War" (288) — he does effectively assess the novel as a (to use Linda Hutcheon's term) historiographic metafiction, a fiction that questions the making of both fiction and history. Hutcheon argues that contemporary Canadian writers find this form particularly attractive because it readily answers both "a post-colonial Canadian need to reclaim the past" and a more general postmodern "need to investigate the ontological nature" of narrative (73). Contesting conventional Canadian historical narrative in order to reclaim a Japanese-Canadian past, Kogawa belongs to this Canadian novelistic tradition:

Certainly, in her use of multiple discursive modes, tenses, and narrative points-of-view — from the soaring lyricism of Naomi's narrative, through the "factual" reportage of Emily's diaries, to the authoritarian, third-person stance of government documents and newspaper articles — Kogawa disrupts and contests the dominant culture's totalizing, omniscient voice of history. (Goellnicht 294)

She does so, Goellnicht also points out, to show that "[t]he historical sources present more fabrication than the novel, yet they also unwittingly reveal an unintended truth: the pervasive racism that . . . we as Canadians have tried for so long to deny" (294). *Obasan* is thus a fiction that tells the truth about the truth that was a fiction that did not hide the truth. . . .

A few critics have focused even more specifically on the problematic narration of the novel as opposed to the problematics of what is narrated. "Since the entire book is a document of silence turning into sound, we become intensely aware of the burden carried by the language in this invocation of the consciousness of a silent people" (Gottlieb 39). Erika Gottlieb examines the extent to which Naomi is "blocked and benumbed" by her past experience, how she must consequently convey much of her meaning through dreams and metaphors, and how "the special flavour of Japanese Canadian speech patterns and their underlying [fatalistic] sensibilities" and silences are worked into the novel (39). From a slightly different and largely Lacanian perspective, Manina Jones also explores these issues in her article "The Avenues of Speech and Silence," as does A. Lynne Magnusson in "Language and Longing in Joy Kogawa's 'Obasan.'" For Magnusson, much in the novel, starting with the prefatory proem, is "indeterminate and, perhaps . . . indeterminable" (59), and is so because of Naomi's past history, and particularly her loss of her mother — a "crisis of separation" that "coincides with [the daughter's] entry into the symbolic order of language" (62). For the general reader who wishes to avoid entanglement with Lacanian analysis, P. Merivale's comparison of *Obasan* and Anne Hébert's *Les fous de Bassan* traces how, in Kogawa especially, "an oblique feminism of marginality" leads to "silence finding a voice" (74).

Other voices besides that of feminism sound in this polyvocal text, but what we hear, unfortunately, depends largely on who we are, as can be seen even in the ethnocentricity of much of the criticism. For Canadian critics, the novel is, not surprisingly, mostly about Canada. Yet Gayle K. Fujita, an American *nikkei* (of Japanese ancestry) critic, identifies the novel's protagonist as a *nikkei*, and does so in an

American context and through comparisons to American texts, while Shirley Geok-Lin Lim, in "Japanese American Women's Life Stories: Maternality in Monica Sone's *Nisei Daughter* and Joy Kogawa's *Obasan*," claims from the beginning American title over Kogawa's Canadian character. Still further afield, a Japanese scholar writing in English (but for a Japanese journal) sees in the novel sad proof that "the ethnic culture of the Japanese-Canadian society" is being diluted "in the mosaic of Canadian literature" (Tsutsumi 109). I would also here note that the novel was published in Japan as *Ushinawareto sokoku*, which might best be translated as "Lost Ancestral Land" (a highly misleading title, but perhaps only from an Occidental perspective).

The tendency of Canadian critics to see the novel as making a statement about Canada also raises questions about Canada. Whose Canada? Obasan's or Mackenzie King's? Which Canada? The Canada that curtailed the liberties and confiscated the property of more than 20,000 Japanese Canadians in 1942? Or the Canada that apologized and paid restitution in 1988? And notice that the belated compensation of 1988 does not put racism totally and safely in the past. Why not insist that full justice finally be done and return as much seized property as possible to its prewar Japanese-Canadian owners or their heirs, leaving those who long profited from the original injustice to bear some of its cost?[3]

The point that I am making is that, even in the Canadian context, *Obasan* is a cross-cultural work that raises questions about perspective. When Gary Willis, for example, in a scrupulously sympathetic reading of the novel, observes that Naomi has no suitable models of womanhood, partly because "Obasan's marriage to Sam, though devoted, is empty of touch and tenderness" (241), he reads too much through Western eyes, taking the absence of the outward sign of a feeling as proof of the absence of that feeling. As Kogawa has noted, "one of the distinguishing features of Japanese culture" is the way that "things going on internally" are often "never exposed" (qtd. in Howells 118). My own rule of thumb, while in Japan, was the inverse equation that the more something mattered privately the less it was shown publicly. So someone who took, say, a Japanese mother or father's "dismissive" comment on an "unfortunate" child as an injustice to the child and a show of parental disregard probably could not be more wrong.

I cite what to me is an obvious misestimation of a marriage not because it is a serious error (it isn't), but because it is an indicative one that warns of the difficulty of reading across cultural differences. A number of *Obasan*'s critics have particularly heeded this difficulty. Gayle K. Fujita, for example, traces the source of the protagonist's final "spiritual triumph" to her *nikkei* heritage and her more traditionally Japanese aunt (40). In a slightly different vein, Ila Goody argues that "*Obasan* stands exactly on the balancing point of two literatures" (145), and explores how those two, Canadian and Japanese, inform this text. Gottlieb notices the "[c]oincidence of Buddhist and Christian symbols" in the novel, and suggests that the joint development of "allusions to the Buddhist and the Biblical tradition" might serve "to demonstrate that elusive ideal of multiculturalism that may offer the narrator hope for the political future" (50).

Thanks to these critics and others, the reader can bring a more "Japanese" perspective to bear on *Obasan* and thus better appreciate the Japanese-Canadian perspective that *Obasan* brings to bear on Canada. From that perspective, Canada begins to become a different Canada. The story of Momotaro, a traditional Japanese children's tale, *is* a Canadian story, one character in the novel insists. And it is, to the degree that *Obasan* also becomes a Canadian story and not just a somehow-marginalized, Japanese-Canadian one.

Which brings me to my last point in this review of the scholarship. There is one major critical task still to be done. The novel has not yet been assessed in any larger context of Canadian ethnic and First Peoples' writing, and neither has that context itself been established for Canada (in the sense, say, that Werner Sollors's *Beyond Ethnicity: Consent and Descent in American Culture* interconnects the United States, ethnicity, and American literature). The main Canadian attempt at some similar endeavour, Arnold Harrichand Itwaru's *The Invention of Canada: Literary Text and the Immigrant Imaginary*, is too much concerned with a *male* "Imaginary," which, for Canada, is particularly dubious. If, as Linda Hutcheon argues, "the periphery or the margin" as "Canada's perceived position" also perfectly situates the Canadian writer for the postmodern task of "undercutting prevailing values and conventions in order to provoke a questioning, a challenging of 'what goes without saying' in our culture" (3), then who better occupies that central and marginal position than the Canadian ethnic woman writer? In books such as *Obasan* and Sky

Lee's *The Disappearing Moon Cafe*, Canadian ethnic writers are masterfully telling their individual stories, but the composite story of those tellings remains to be told.[4]

Reading of the Text

The novel itself is preceded by three brief passages that partly presage and partly foreground the literary tasks confronting, first, the author of *Obasan*, then the narrator/protagonist of the novel, and, finally, the reader perusing Naomi Nakone's unfolding story as written by Joy Kogawa. Not surprisingly, these three tasks turn out to be only slightly different versions of much the same enterprise, the making of story from silence. Joy Kogawa, on the broadest level, sets out to write a novel detailing the experience of Canadians of Japanese ancestry during World War II and after. It is a painful story of the country's failure, of its fall into a lesser version of the very evil that ostensibly justified the war against Nazism. Not surprisingly, it is also a story that Canada would prefer not to hear. To tell that story, to keep it from becoming an unfortunate past event best (best for whom?) forgotten, Kogawa creates a protagonist whose personal life mirrors the social and historical focus of the novel. That protagonist, grown to adulthood, embodies the consequences of her own and her family's past suffering in Canada and, try as she might to deny and repress that heritage, she finally finds that it is her own life for which she must account. Moreover, Naomi's engagement with her story, and her making narration out of silence and suffering, also requires the reader to become involved with that same story and particularly prompts a crucial question. Considering how the injustices perpetrated against Japanese Canadians were both justified and resisted, where would we, as individual readers, have stood? Equally to the point, where do we, as individuals in a still-imperfect world, stand? For Naomi's story is also our story, a story of who we were and of who we still might be.

To forge an articulate story out of a largely silenced history requires, first, a heeding of the history on which the text is based. The novel, in short, cannot be conventionally fictional, merely a made-up story. Consider, in this context, the simplest of the three prefatory passages, the author's disclaimer, acknowledgement, and dedication. Here Kogawa writes in her own voice of the text that she has presumably completed and that the reader is about to commence. She first notes that "[a]lthough this novel is based on historical events, and many of the persons named are real, most of the characters are fictional." This is not quite the standard and often-suspect authorial claim that any resemblance between the fictional characters here portrayed and actual persons, living or dead, is purely coincidental. Kogawa insists on the factuality of her fiction. Although Naomi's own story is not literally true, the experience portrayed in the novel happened. It involved "many" people, and "many" of them are named in the text. That same point about the truth of the narrative is also emphasized when Kogawa goes on to thank various individuals and "the Public Archives of Canada, for permission to use documents and letters from the files of Muriel Kitagawa, Grace Tucker, T. Buck Suzuki and Gordon Nakayama." The history on which this novel is based is documented in the Public Archives. If you doubt it, you can check it out yourself.

The calculated implications of both *public* and *archives* are only part of Kogawa's intent in here acknowledging some of her sources. Muriel Kitagawa, Grace Tucker, T. Buck Suzuki, and Gordon Nakayama are not just witnesses, they are also significantly named witnesses. What name, for example, could be more conventionally English Canadian than Grace Tucker? Similarly, T. Buck hardly attests to a Japanese identity, and Muriel is itself a badge of assimilation. Given the difficulties Japanese speakers commonly have with the Western *r* and *l*, such names become shibboleths in that "Muriel," properly pronounced (as opposed to "Mulier"), effectively demonstrates a successful linguistic crossing. So one point of the names is to set forth the Canadian identity of those they designated and the very impossibility of denying, as Canada tried to do, that salient fact.

The author then concludes her brief prefatory statement by dedicating the book "to my mother and father and to those amazing people, the Issei — the few who are still with us and those who have gone." The second term of this dedication, the *Issei* (the first generation of Japanese immigrants to live in Canada), evokes the late-nineteenth-century arrival of Japanese immigrants in British Columbia, the long history of discrimination they there encountered, and the crisis precipitated by the outbreak of war with Japan.[5] Their story is being lost as they die; their deaths are reflected in the text by the demise of the protagonist's grandparents and parents. Such deaths represent another source of silence in the novel, but this silence, too, must be told, sounded. Moreover, the naming of the first generation *Issei* and the counting of the generations as generations away from Japan — *Issei, Nisei* (second generation), *Sansei* (third generation) — evinces a Japanese tendency for careful ranking and order, and so runs counter to the implications of the Anglo first names. Muriel Kitagawa was a "Muriel," but she was also a "Kitagawa." Yet the fact that she had such a second name, I would here insist, hardly meant that she merited being sent to a concentration camp (not that she would have been kept from one by the still more Anglicized name of Muriel Northriver). As the novel makes clear, citizens of Germany and Italy residing in Canada were not automatically regarded as security threats, whereas Canadians of Japanese ancestry were.

The hint of the silence of death at the end of the author's acknowledgement and dedication might explain its odd placing between the two epigraphs, which both sound, in different ways, a more sustained note of silence. The first, taken from the Bible, is brief enough to be reproduced in its entirety:

To him that overcometh
will I give to eat
of the hidden manna
and will give him
a white stone
and in the stone
a new name written. . . .

Printed as poetry, this passage (from Rev. 2.17) promises both sustenance and survival. But as the manna provided by the Lord gives way to the white stone He also gives, and as the stone provides a new name, the biblical passage "in the beginning was the word" is transmuted into "in the end is the word," even though that final, crucial word, the new name, written *in* the stone, not on it, does not loudly proclaim itself.

The second epigraph, presumably the protagonist's poetic prose musing on the narrative she is about to recount, even more obviously foregrounds silence — the two silences, in fact, that will loom large in her story — both the silence of her missing mother and the silence of others, especially the aunt (*obasan* is the Japanese word for aunt) who raised her without telling her the full story of the mother's absence and death. "There is a silence [the mother] that cannot speak," it begins, "There is a silence [Obasan] that will not speak." This pervasive double silence soon leads to a passage that explicitly invokes the biblical epigraph with its hints of silence: "The word is stone," and "[u]nless the stone bursts with telling . . . there is in my life no living word." "[S]ound," the second epigraph continues, "is only sound," and words "are pock marks on the earth. . . . are hailstones seeking an underground stream." The speaker does wonder if she might follow the hailstones to the underground stream, "to the hidden voice," and "come at last to the freeing word." But when she puts this question to the night sky, "the silence is steadfast," and, in the last words of this poetic passage, "[t]here is no reply." Despite the distinct possibility of speech introduced by the opening difference between "cannot" and "will not," and despite the possibility of coming "at last to the freeing word," what we encounter here is a mostly pervasive silence extending from high in the heavens to deep in the earth. It is against this silence that the novel must be told, must become its own "reply." In a sense, the narrator's dialogue with the universe has been reduced to vain monologue and even, as she stands attending that final "no reply," to silence. Somehow the process needs to be reversed. Silence has to be succeeded by monologue again, and monologue by dialogue, which is precisely what happens as the narrator recounts the novel. That process, not coincidentally, is also predicted in the epigraphs, particularly by the "stone" connection between them. Even when the word is stone, that stone can still flower into speech, revealing the word, the name, previously entombed within it.

The biblical provenance of the first epigraph and the biblical undertones of the second both promise something more than "steadfast" stasis and silence. Indeed, one of the "underground streams" of the second epigraph is the dialogical implications of its biblical subtext. As the speaker affirms that "[t]he word is stone" and acknowledges that "I hate the stillness. I hate the stone. I hate the sealed vault with its cold icon," that conjunction of a stone and a sealed vault, particularly in the presence of a cold icon, emphasizes the larger Christian iconography of the whole passage. Stones can be rolled away. New life, new beginnings, can be born from the grave. Through the very wording of this passage, the trope of resurrection takes precedence over the trope of entombment, and thus the stone itself can speak "the living word" in a Christian sense.

Although that stone can set forth the Christian word, the way to this word is not totally Christian: "Beneath the grass the speaking dreams and beneath the dreams is a sensate sea. That speech that frees comes forth from that amniotic deep. To attend its voice, I can hear it say, is to embrace its absence. But I fail the task. The word is stone." Later in the novel, it will become clear that the buried "sensate sea" as a kind of "amniotic deep" is, in part, a reference to the mother now dead on the other side of the Pacific Ocean, and it is the missing mother's voice that the speaker both hears and does not hear. The indeterminate absence and presence of that hearing/not hearing suggests contemporary poststructural theories of both narrative and personality. Yet Zen Buddhism predates deconstruction by many centuries, and the narrative contradiction of hearing a voice say that it can be heard only when it is not heard is not so much a Derridean demonstration of the instability of narrative as a Zen koan (a verbal statement aimed at prompting an enlightenment beyond the realm of words — for example, a question such as "What is the sound of no voice speaking?"). "Beneath the grass the speaking dreams" as a reference to the continued presence of the dead and the Buddhist, not the Christian, interplay of life and death is also suggested by the echo in that passage of one of the poet Basho's most famous haiku: "The summer grasses — / of brave soldiers' dreams / The aftermath" (369).[6]

Even the title of the book embodies this bicultural context. *Obasan* is obviously not an English word. Just as obviously, it is not written in *kanji* (the ideogram characters the Japanese early borrowed from the Chinese) nor in *hiragana* or *katagana* (Japan's two subsequent indigenous syllabaries). The title manages, at one and the same time, to be neither English nor Japanese, to be both English and Japanese. *Obasan*, as the Japanese word for *aunt*, also has an appropriately double and divided reference in the novel itself. The protagonist, her mother missing and then dead, is situated between two aunts, each from a different side of her family, and each embodying a different aspect of the family's Japanese-Canadian heritage. Obasan is by far the more traditionally Japanese of the two; Aunt Emily, in partial recognition of her determination to be Canadian, not Japanese, is always called *Aunt* Emily; yet she, too, is Obasan just as Obasan is Aunt.

The semantic interconnections of *obasan* and *aunt* (similarity and difference in a nutshell), like the merging of biblical and Buddhist implications in the two epigraphs, demonstrate the interplay of different cultural contexts that runs throughout *Obasan*, starting even with the opening episode. The first words spoken in the novel come as the narrator, Naomi Nakane, and her uncle pay an annual visit to a prairie coulee outside the town where Obasan and Uncle (note that the names are in different languages) now live: " 'Nothing changes ne,' I say as we walk towards the rise" (1). *Ne* is a Japanese sentence marker roughly analogous to *ka*, which, at the end of any sentence, turns the preceding statement into a question. But *ne* does not really question the truth of the statement it follows; instead, it solicits the listener's agreement with that statement by posing a question and already implicitly answered in the affirmative. The nearest English equivalent of *ne* is the Canadian *eh*, as in "you agree with me, eh?" In a small touch of brilliance, the first Japanese word in the novel is not translated nor, especially for Canadian readers, need it be.

"Nothing changes ne," Naomi asks, because, from her perspective, nothing has changed. The novel begins with Naomi and her uncle making the same nighttime pilgrimage to a quiet prairie coulee that they have made, readers are early informed, for 18 years. The coulee remains the same, a break in a stretch of virgin land where the grass has not been cut since "the beginning of time" (2). The opening visit is dated 9 August 1972; the first such visit took place in August of 1954 when Naomi was 18, so for half her life she has come on this annual excursion, yet she still does not know the significance of the trip or of the timing. "Uncle . . . why do we come here every year?" (3), she asks, presumably for the eighteenth time, and once more he does not answer her, but comments, as he always does, on the waving grass: "Umi no yo. . . . It's like the sea" (1). And every visit "always" ends with Naomi leaving her uncle and descending into the coulee, to where wild roses "cluster along the edges of the trickle" that seeps from an underground stream, where she picks "at least one flower before [going] home" (4).

29

In its repetitiveness, this annual ceremony denies change and denies even the fact that Uncle is becoming, as he acknowledges on what will prove to be his final visit to the coulee, "[t]oo much old man" (1). But in its symbolism it affirms the devastating changes that have befallen the protagonist and her family. There is first the matter of the date of the visit, which is the first detail provided in the novel. As a few readers will probably recognize, and as all will later be reminded, 9 August is the day the second atomic bomb was dropped on Japan. Naomi also eventually discovers that her lost mother, trapped in Japan during the war, was in Nagasaki during the summer of 1945 and not, as the family believed, in Tokyo. The mother survived the blast but was horribly mutilated, and decided not to inflict her tragedy on her children by returning to them or telling them of her fate. Consequently, the uncle and the two aunts, "for the sake of the children" (a phrase that runs like a refrain through the novel), never acknowledged the real reasons for the mother's continuing absence. "Too young. . . . Still too young" (3), Uncle had said when they first visited the coulee, soon after he had been informed of the mother's death, almost a decade after the war had ended. Ostensibly still too young 18 years later, Naomi has not yet been told that the yearly visits commemorate the fate of her mother. Nevertheless, on some level she knows — or at least suspects — what she, and her uncle, cannot articulate. For the flower she "always" takes back with her is picked in symbolic mourning for her missing mother. Moreover, when, at the bottom, she "stand[s] for a long time watching as the contours of the coulee erode slowly in the night" (4), that complex image of decay, disappearance, and descending darkness sums up the sense of loss that characterizes her life, as does the coulee itself, a rupture in the sea of grass.

Naomi is not the only one imaged in loss. Her "[n]othing changes ne" is followed immediately by her uncle's annual observation on the waving grass — "Umi no yo. . . . It's like the sea" — which is also, as Naomi recognizes, "the closest Uncle [now] ever gets to the ocean" (2). In his conjoined Japanese/English formulation, he reenvisions the life he has lost at the edge of and on the Pacific, the oceangoing heritage of his ancestors, and the boats he lovingly built. So the annual visit, like Uncle's regular baking of his almost inedible "stone bread" (analogous to Dante's bitter bread of exile), is a ceremony of exile, and every August he commemorates not just the fate of Naomi's mother but the whole family's misfortunes in Canada.

It should be noted, however, that the novel's dominant note of loss is, from the first, also regularly muted. When the uncle, for example, once encountered fossilized sea shells on the prairie, he marvelled that the ocean had covered the land he now worked. When he sees the sea figuratively present in the waving grass he partly recovers the earlier life from which he has been exiled. "Itsuka, mata itsuka. Someday, someday again," Naomi remembers her uncle saying in the sugar-beet fields. "He was waiting for that 'some day' when he could go back to the boats," is her reading of this comment. "But he never did" (22). In another sense, however, he always did. Neither are Uncle's stone loaves totally the bread of exile. The very difficulty of eating them connects them with *mochi*, cakes of pounded glutinous rice traditionally served in Japan as part of the New Year celebration, and notoriously difficult to consume. When Uncle bakes his first bread, Naomi asks, "How can you eat that stone? ... It'll break your teeth" (13), and her first mention of *mochi* prompts her to observe that "Obasan eats it without her false teeth, ever since the time the mochi clamped her teeth together so tight she had to soak them in hot water for hours" (20). Naomi's reference to Uncle's bread as "stone" recalls, too, the previously quoted first epigraph, and hints that one possible reading of that elliptical biblical passage might derive from seeing the "white stone" as a kind of bread/*mochi*. "To him that overcometh [anyone who can consume the stuff] will I give to eat of the hidden manna" could then suggest both the well-disguised nourishment of this unpalatable food as well as its symbolic significance in both a Japanese (the cycling of time) and a Western (the staff of life) context.

The significance of the timing of the annual coulee excursion also carries implications of the initial 9 August date. When Naomi observes that "[w]e come here once every year around this time" (1), not once every year on this specific day, she partly separates the annual event from its Nagasaki reference. And saying "around this time," sometime towards the middle of August, does allow for another evocative Japanese reference. O-Bon, the Japanese Buddhist festival of the dead and a major traditional ceremony, has been celebrated in Japan since the end of World War II from 13 August through 15 August. On the first day, the dead are honoured by their families at their grave sites and then, "[a]s darkness sets," they are called back home again to share briefly in the world of the living, to be served tiny portions of ceremonial and favourite foods, to take part in "imagined conversation . . . as real [to the living participants] as any actual affair of the moment," before, on the night of the last day, being lighted by "farewell fires" back to *Meido*, the Celestial World of Darkness." On that last night the family also puts small lanterns or lit candles along with burning incense in tiny straw boats, "which [are] floated on a running stream or cast on the sea — both methods as a means of comforting those who have no grave but the river or the ocean bed" (*We Japanese* 60). There is no ocean in Alberta but the waving grass; no stream but the "surface seepage" in the coulee; no incense but the smell of the roses growing along the edge of that "trickle"; no lantern or candles but the new moon and "[t]he whole dark sky . . . bright with stars" (1); nevertheless, the annual August evening ceremony is, especially for Uncle, a truncated O-Bon, a one-night hail and farewell that mourns the tragic death of a sister-in-law in Japan even as it commemorates the abiding links between the living and the dead.

FIGURING THE PAST

As the novel opens, it is precisely those links with the dead Naomi does not yet know or adequately acknowledge. Her ignorance and innocence allow her to deny death by claiming that nothing changes, an assertion that her uncle obliquely questions by pointing to his own impending mortality. Appropriately, death will soon teach her the facts of life, and begins to do so in the second chapter, dated just a little over a month after the opening August visit to the coulee. On 13 September, word comes to her at the school where she teaches, some 150 miles from Granton, that her uncle has passed away. That death brings her back to Granton to comfort Obasan and to begin to confront her own past, particularly the deaths, the losses, the changes she has hitherto tried to downplay. At first the confrontation takes the form of reminiscence. Thus, hearing Obasan describe how Uncle died, she can see a last, fresh loaf of his bread, wonder if the baking of it was his final act, and remember the whole history of that hard fare.

But even as she dwells on the imagined details of his dying — "What, I wonder, was Uncle thinking those last few hours? Had the world turned upside down?" — her formulations strike an unconsciously personal note. For example, in the same passage, she goes on to imagine him "tunnelling backwards" and "groping down . . . to the damp cellar, to the water, down to the underground sea" (14). That "underground sea" suggests the buried "sensate sea" of the second epigraph as well as both sides of the Pacific. So Uncle, in dying, could have gone "back to his fishing boats in B.C.," and perhaps even farther: "In the end did he manage to swim full circle back to that other shore and his mother's arms, her round moon face glowing down at her firstborn?" (14). Of course Naomi, too, needs to be reunited with a mother now dead on that distant "other shore."

Naomi partly confronts — and partly evades — the immediacy of her uncle's death by contextualizing it within a review of the family's fate in Canada. Such exposition conveniently provides the reader with the larger history in which Naomi's story occurs. For example, when she recalls how Grandpa Nakane, the first grandparent to come to Canada from Japan, arrived in 1893, "wearing a western suit, round black hat, and platformed geta on his feet" (18), those shoes, especially, show that he is less than fully accoutered for a new and different life. Later, in Canada, his family, sent first to Slocan and then to the sugar-beet fields in Alberta, will follow in his footsteps. In other ways, too, the early history of the family typifies what is to come. After Grandpa Nakane marries a cousin's widowed wife who had emigrated from Japan with her son, Isami, he takes that son into the family boat-building business. When Isami is grown and married, he and his wife take in and raise their niece and nephew. Both these cases of taking others in contrast with Canada's attempt to exclude the Japanese. Or when the two children of Isami and his wife die at birth, that double loss anticipates Naomi and Stephen's loss of both their parents and the consequent merging of the two families maimed in inverse fashion.

Such historical contextualizing is also, in part, an attempt to remember a happy time before the family was fractured and dispersed. Finding that the father's side does not really serve this objective, Naomi turns to the mother's, which works no better. Her father, Uncle Sam's younger half-brother, had married one of the two daughters born to Doctor Kato, who, with his wife, also emigrated from Japan. The elder of the two Kato sisters, delicate and beautiful, becomes Naomi's mother; the younger, her Aunt Emily, is short and

33

stocky, and never marries. There is also another significant difference between the two sisters. Starting when Grandpa Kato was a medical student, his wife would regularly leave him with one of the daughters, Emily, and take the other with her to visit her family in Japan. On the basis of this periodic separation, Naomi "wonder[s] if the Katos were ever really a happy family" (20), and again there is a more personal relevance to her question than she is ready to admit. Much later, Naomi's mother was still accompanying Grandma Kato on those trips to Japan, and leaving her own husband and children to do so. Even though Naomi never asks if her parents were ever really happy, she must wonder about her place and value in this scheme of things that apparently required a woman's responsibilities to her mother to take precedence over her responsibilities to her daughter.

Although Naomi tries to cast her parents as the "two needles [that] knit the [Kato and Nakane] families carefully into one blanket" (20), she immediately acknowledges that the figurative blanket has "become badly moth-eaten with time" (21). Indeed, this tenuous figure is soon literalized when Naomi and Obasan, searching in the attic, come across the patchwork quilt Naomi's mother had made for her when she was four, now "so frayed and moth-eaten it's only a rag" (25). Moreover, just as we soon find out that no real or metaphoric blanket fully protected Naomi as a child, we also immediately learn that the family could not shelter its members in the new world to which they had come. Sheltering, in fact, marked defeat. Aunt Emily, for example, had the highest grades at the teachers college she attended but "was unable to get a teaching position and stayed home to help Grandpa Kato with his medical practice" (21). Naomi's father went to university, but entered the Nakane boat-building business and devoted his considerable artistic talents to designing and helping to build an especially "sleek boat" that particularly impressed the police when they seized it in 1941. "What a beauty" (21), the RCMP officer repeatedly exclaimed as he took the boat away, shortly before Uncle himself was also taken away with the Canadian-Japanese fishermen and their confiscated fishing fleet.

We are not told why careers were closed off to the father or the aunt, nor need we be. The final detail of the seizing of the boat — of all the boats — lands us squarely in the racial politics of British Columbia, which came to a crisis with the outbreak of the war. When Naomi, right after recalling these details, claims, "[t]he memories were drowned in a whirlpool of protective silence" (21) (silence both past and present), we need not believe her. Even the details she has just provided, not to mention the silence of the missing mother, attest that silence does not protect. Not surprisingly, much of the rest of the novel will be a plumbing of the silence Naomi has hitherto attempted to assert.

"Just a glimpse of a worn-out patchwork quilt and the old question comes thudding out of the night again like a giant moth. Why did my mother not return?" (26). If the ragged blanket literalizes the frayed state of the family and Naomi's problematic relationship to her past, the discovery of that blanket also literalizes the process whereby Naomi might begin to resolve some of her quandaries, even though she does not initially see it that way. The blanket is found when, on her first night back in Granton, Naomi awakens after midnight to find Obasan searching the house with a flashlight and muttering the Japanese word for *lost*, which is also the word for *dead*. Naomi helps her aunt up the steep stairs to the attic, where the blanket along with other suggestive items are found — Grandfather Nakane's woodworking tools, Uncle's wartime identity card, "a whole cloudy scene of [spiders' webs and spiders'] carnage" (25). Naomi symbolically reads the unfolding scene as validating what might be termed "the rule of the attic." "Everything, I suppose, turns to dust eventually," she muses, and "[a] man's memories end up in some attic," while "his face is lost in fading photographs" (25). In much the same vein, she sees herself and Obasan "trapped" in that literal and metaphoric attic "by our memories of the dead — all our dead — those who refuse to bury themselves. Like threads of old spider webs, still sticky and hovering, the past waits for us to submit, or depart" (26). The first burden of the past is this sense of it as a hovering stickiness that holds everything and gives up nothing — the aftermath of spiders' feasts. Furthermore, the persistent insect imagery effectively denies human will, human inquiry. What can a question that "comes thudding out of the night [and the past] like a giant moth" do but entangle itself in a waiting web? Seeing the past this way, Naomi has learned not to ask. Indeed, she was once "devoured" and "consumed" by questions about what had happened to her mother and what her mother was like, questions that Obasan, at the time, could not or would not answer. Later Obasan seems even less likely to provide answers: "Everything is forgetfulness" (26), she repeats as she continues her search, despite having apparently forgotten just what it is she seeks.

Naomi's "attic philosophy" of the past admits four basic possibilities. One can shut oneself up in it as Obasan has apparently done — "The past hungers for her. Feasts on her. And when its feasting is complete? She will dance and dangle in the dark, like small insect bones" (26). One can follow Naomi's brother Stephen's course and flee it completely, or at least as completely as possible. One can use it as a convenient junk room where anything not presently useful can be consigned, out of sight and hopefully out of mind (as Canada has mostly done with the story of the Japanese in Canada, and as Naomi has attempted to do up to this point in the novel). Or one can view it as a repository that allows and requires ordering, sorting (as Aunt Emily has compulsively done and as Naomi will do for much of the rest of the novel). The significant change for Naomi comes, moreover, partly because what Obasan had searched for was neither forgotten nor lost. It was not even in the attic but in the kitchen, a different symbolism entirely. What Obasan finds the next morning is a parcel from Aunt Emily, "as heavy as a loaf of Uncle's stone bread" (31). The burden of the past and the figuring of that burden has already markedly shifted.

The parcel contains mostly family papers, old newspaper clippings, and Aunt Emily's private journal. But what first catches Naomi's attention is a single sheet that falls out of the package as she is opening it. In her aunt's spidery and almost illegible handwriting, a brief biblical passage — "Write the vision and make it plain" (31; the passage is from Hab. 2.2) — has been set down as an exhortation, possibly for Aunt Emily herself, possibly for Naomi. Naomi, however, first sees this quotation as embodying "the truth" as her aunt "lives it": "When she is called like Habakkuk to the witness stand, her testimony is to the light that shines in the lives of the Nisei, in their desperation to prove themselves Canadian, in their tough and gentle spirit." For Naomi, "[t]he truth . . . is more murky, shadowy and grey" (32).

Just how much more murky Naomi's "truth" might be has already been suggested in the novel by a dream she had the previous night, after having assisted in the futile midnight attic search. It is a puzzling dream, the hazy details of which emerge "from out of another dream or from nowhere," and seem as "indistinct as the fog" (28). Never-

36

theless, Naomi can still recount this dream in which a man and a woman (vaguely herself) come upon, in a forest, another couple, the woman (Obasan) the embodiment of work, and the man (a British officer) the pattern of rule. Even though they "do not know what [it] is" (29), the couple join in the work, which is endlessly, timelessly wearying. But a change comes when a huge and wonderfully obedient lion or dog, or lion dog, in the service of the officer proves to be a plastic robot, and the dream then ends with Uncle, a rose in his mouth, enacting a ritual dance of the dead, while "[b]ehind him, someone — I do not know who — is straining to speak" (30). At this point, all is again lost in a cloud. Clearly, the pervasive cloud and mist in this anxiety dream suggest the continuing uncertainty of Naomi herself. Some of the grounds of that uncertainty are also hinted at in the dream. More specifically, the final figure "straining to speak" is most likely the long-dead mother. If so, she is now conjoined with the uncle through both silence and death. Furthermore, the mother's continuing speechlessness, like the uncle's silent dance — his silence strikingly marked by the "red red rose with an endless stem" he holds in his mouth (30) — alludes back to the second epigraph's "unless the seed flowers with speech, there is in my life no living word," and to the coulee ceremony (during which a rose is picked), as well. Other dream details are also relevant. The endless forest labour is an amalgam of the hard life first in the camps of the British Columbia interior and then later in the Alberta sugar-beet fields, while the "British martinet" embodies the anglocentric policies of Canada that consigned the Japanese to those double displacements.

More tenuously, the lion dog — the traditional guardian of a Japanese temple, here in the service of a British officer — might suggest to what degree Japanese values emphasizing obedience and order were co-opted by the government of Canada and used against Japanese Canadians. This could partly explain why the lion dog proves false (a plastic robot), and why the moment of recognizing that fakery is, in the dream, so liberating. "[A] house of cards silently collapses. Instantly in our telepathic world, the knowing spreads and the great boulder enclosing change splits apart" (29). Is "change" itself thus the "new name" that is written "in the stone" (the first epigraph) and the "living word" provided when "the stone bursts with telling" (the second epigraph)? Of course other interpretations of this highly symbolic dream could be advanced, which is to say that there is a significant difference between dreaming the vision and writing it, between writing it and making it plain. Naomi's crucial dream/vision is hardly plain either for her or for the reader at this point in the narrative.

Again Naomi proceeds by indirection. Instead of making plain how the biblical dictum on making it plain might apply to her, she assesses Aunt Emily's commitment to this same counsel and thereby explicitly contrasts her two aunts. "One lives in sound, the other in stone." Whereas "Obasan's language remains deeply underground," Aunt Emily is "a word warrior. . . . a crusader, a little old grey-haired Mighty Mouse, a Bachelor of Advanced Activists and General Practitioner of Just Causes" (32). Such piling up of increasingly loquacious characterizations implicitly — and rather hypocritically — questions the efficacy of words. It also smacks of evasion as does, too, Naomi's next ploy, which is to turn away from the writing Aunt Emily has sent to reconstruct in detail her last visit with this same aunt.

Naomi's privileging of the past spoken word over the present written one permits a certain degree of textual exposition whereby the social and historical context of the novel is made clearer for the reader, just as earlier the family context was. Aunt Emily, Naomi can conveniently remember, had emphasized on her last visit the ways in which the suffering of Japanese Canadians was worse than that of Japanese Americans. She had stressed the incongruity of not considering most German nationals to be security threats when even Canadian citizens of Japanese descent supposedly were. Just back from a conference on the Japanese diaspora in North America, she thrusts on her niece a paper on the Orwellian use of language: "prisons," for example, become "Interior Housing Projects." "With language like that," she rightly observed, "you can disguise any crime" (34).[7] Aunt Emily had Naomi read the callous bureaucratic letter that "B. Good," the custodian of confiscated property, wrote to "advise" Emily that because her mother was "a Japanese National living in Japan at the outbreak of war, all property belonging to her in Canada [that is, the family house] vests in the Custodian" (37), and a newspaper clipping quoting the prime minister's sleazy yet self-congratulatory rationalization for denying Canadians of Japanese descent the vote. "There would have been riots at the polls," Mackenzie King claims, "and certainly it was taking the part of wisdom to see that nothing of the kind should take place" (41).

Recalling Aunt Emily's last visit, Naomi also remembers how she herself was called upon to defend her own perspective on the past. "There were a number of people at the conference," Aunt Emily noted, "who were cautioning against 'rocking the boat'" (35). Naomi would have been one of those people, but is reluctant to even say so. Appropriately, it is this reluctance to take a stand (including even the stand of acknowledged disinterest) that brings Naomi, five months later, the "burden" of the whole parcel. "I'll send you some of my correspondence and stuff. Would you like that?", Aunt Emily asked, at the very end of this last visit. Naomi's answer: "'Sure,' I lied" (43).

Naomi's recalling of her aunt's visit is a covert attempt to put a concern with the past safely in the past that simply does not work. She is constructing history to avoid constructing history, and much the same contradiction runs through the history, the memory, she here reconstructs. Thus Naomi recalls that, confronting her forceful aunt, "[t]he very last thing in the world I was interested in talking about was our experiences during and after World War II" (33). She would prefer to let "[c]rimes of history . . . stay in history," and would "leave the dead to bury the dead" (41, 42). Yet she has hardly consigned her dead mother to that oblivion. Furthermore, when she read the letter about the confiscation of her grandmother's house, her interest was palpable and immediate. She bitterly noted the "be obedient, be servile, above all don't send me any letters of enquiry about your homes" subtext of this communication (37), and she wondered, in a brief passage that effectively evokes Hannah Arendt's treatise on the banality of evil, what Mr. B. Good might have felt as he wrote such letters. "Did he experience a tiny twinge of pleasure at the power his signature must represent? Did [he] sometimes imagine himself to be God? Or was it all just a day's mindless job?" (37). B. Good as a minor A. Eichmann? Such questions contradict Naomi's assertion that she lied when she claimed interest.

Concerned with the parcel again, Naomi tries to think, in the novel's present, about what she has just recalled thinking in the past, and again it does not work. "What is past recall is past pain," she maintains, overlooking just how much pain still persists. She continues, in much the same vein but on a more immediate level, to insist that "[q]uestions from all these papers" need not disturb "the delicate ecology of this numb day" (45). Yet the very next item from the parcel that seizes Naomi's attention is an ominously familiar folder. It contains two letters on lined blue rice paper written in Japanese, which she asks Obasan to translate for her (Naomi can speak but cannot read Japanese). Obasan rummages for her glasses and a magnifying glass, slowly reads the letters, but will not say who they are from or what they are about. The drawn-out description of her reading, along with her emphatic refusal to answer either of Naomi's questions other than by repeating an often-voiced phrase, "Everyone someday dies" (45), is more than enough to disturb the day. Nor is the disturbance dispelled when Obasan, in lieu of an answer, leaves the room and returns with a photograph, insisting: "Here is the best letter. This is the best time. These are the best memories" (46). Much more than Aunt Emily's package, this photograph sends Naomi tumbling into her past.

THE SUFFERING CHILD

"Only fragments relate me to them now, to this young woman, my mother, and me, her infant daughter," Naomi muses, looking at the photograph Obasan has shown her. "Fragments of fragments. . . . Segments of stories" (53). Appropriately enough, one of the first recovered partial fragments is, indeed, a segment of a story. "Mukashi mukashi," Obasan exclaims over the same photo, and that Japanese equivalent of "a very long time ago" takes Naomi back to her earliest memories and to the favourite story told and retold to her from the time even "before [she] could talk" (54). It is a classic Japanese "fairy tale," the story of Momotaro, the child born from a peach (*momo* in Japanese) and raised by a childless old couple. She particularly recalls her childish sense of wonder at the miraculous birth of the little boy who, "golden and round as a peach, leaps onto the table from the heart of the fruit before [the] astonished eyes" of the old couple who will be his foster parents. "The story could end here," she would think, "but Mother offers the whole telling before she rolls up the tale once more, round and complete as an unopened peach ready for a fresh feasting" (55).

Mother may offer the whole telling. Naomi, however, does not, and the possible significance of this omission was not brought home to me until I taught *Obasan* in Japan to students fully familiar with the tale not fully told. For the miraculous birth prefigures, of course, an appropriately important life, and Momotaro grows up to become a cultural hero who defeats foreign demons and captures their treasure. Moreover, *oni*, the word for foreign demons in "Momotaro," my older Japanese students in an alumnae class informed me, was applied to Caucasians before and during World War II. Is the protagonist of this peach of a tale the hero as conquering jingoist? What I am here suggesting is that the story of Momotaro evokes — and inverts — the larger subject of the novel but does so only for readers who already know the story. They can be reminded that Japan has its forms of racism too. Other readers, however, need no such prompting. For them the issue is not Japanese racism but North American racism directed against the Japanese. But in a joint Japanese/Canadian context, Momotaro's enterprise does bear an uncomfortable similarity to Mackenzie King sanctioning the seizure of "enemy" property, and the resemblance would be even closer had the prime minister, after the war, been able to enforce fully his orders in council that would have sent Japanese Canadians back to Japan where they could be, indeed, dispossessed *foreign* demons. In this sense, Aunt Emily was more right than she knew when she insisted that "Momotaro [was] a Canadian story" (57).

The tale of Momotaro effectively illustrates what we might call the interculturality of texts (the traditional Japanese children's story itself as well as the Canadian novel that partly contains it) and the different reference that the same tale or detail can have in different cultural contexts. But the Momotaro fairy tale functions in the novel in still another way. Not only does it partly predict how Naomi's family will be treated in Canada, but it also anticipates her consequent separation from both her parents. Although the old couple who raise the boy stand in the place of parents, they are not in the story named as his parents but are instead called Grandfather and Grandmother. They thus parallel another older couple who are not named as parents as they raise a child not biologically their own. And again Aunt Emily speaks more truthfully than she knows. "What a serious baby [you were]," she tells Naomi, "fed on milk and Momotaro" (57). It is almost as if the baby all along suspected that the story on which she was raised would become the story of her raising.[8]

The story of Momotaro, moreover, is immediately followed by two other parables of displaced parenthood. The first of these is another of Naomi's early memories. Her parents had purchased a dozen yellow chicks; they also kept a white hen in a cage. When Naomi decides that the birds belong together and puts the chicks into the hen's cage, the hen starts pecking them to death. As the colour symbolism rather obviously suggests, the white hen corresponds to Canada and the yellow chicks to the Japanese who were not taken care of by the foster-mother country and who later will be labelled cowardly (yellow) and weak (the Yellow Peril game, in which three blue kings can defeat fifty yellow pawns) as well. It might also be noted that the first chick attacked went first to the hen, and although this detail with its possible implications is not particularly fore-grounded in the hen-and-chicks episode, a similar situation does figure more prominently in a problematically fragmentary parallel story of mistreatment by a sham parental figure that Naomi imme-diately goes on to tell.

The daughter remembers the calm, matter-of-fact way in which her mother dealt with the baby chick crisis, and how, with that manner, she acknowledged and protected "what is hidden most deeply in the heart of the child" (59). The mother determined, without assigning blame, what had happened and what lesson could be learned from that painful experience: " 'Kyotsuke nakattara abunai,' she says. 'If there is not carefulness, there is danger' " (60). Even the indirection of the language helps to allay Naomi's guilt and allows her to tell her mother "everything." As she concludes: "There is nothing about me that my mother does not know, nothing that is not safe to tell" (60). That conclusion is hardly the whole story, however. As the brief excerpt just quoted illustrates, much of the novel is narrated in an odd tense, a kind of past-present and present-past whereby the time of action melds into the time of narration in an attempt to erase the intervening time, which really cannot be annulled. In this interplay of what are, necessarily, imperfectly merged perspectives, the adult narrator too well knows that the child's formulation of perfect union and trust proved radically untrue and was, furthermore, untrue for the child too. And thus Naomi's large claim of the mother knowing all, being told all, is immediately qualified: "Except there is the one secret thing that emerges even now" like a question seeking "answers still hidden from me" (61). That secret thing is the sexual abuse inflicted on her by Old Man Gower who lived next door, just beyond the peach tree, but who obviously did not "[a]t all times . . . act with

[the] fine intent" that the tale of Momotaro demanded (56).

The abuse began when Naomi was four. Old Man Gower came upon her playing, observed that her knee was scratched, and insisted that "he will fix it for [her]." To dress the injury, a "scratch [that] is hardly visible and does not hurt" (63), he took her into his house, locked the two of them into the bathroom, and started to undress her. Naomi does not fully describe just what then happened, and her accounts of subsequent episodes are similarly inconclusive. The significant point, however, is not to what extent sexual exploitation was actually carried, but that it occurred at all. Furthermore, the very fact that it occurred has no doubt caused a substantial degree of denial and repression, which partly explains the blocked and tentative tone of Naomi's retrospective account. But more telling than her tone is his. We see the pervasive hypocrisy of his pretended concern, the way his "permit me do this for you" does not disguise his real meaning — that she is required to do something for him. Furthermore, his self-proclaimed role as a kind of parental protector is mirrored in the text by such formulations as Mackenzie King's claim that denying Japanese Canadians the vote is really done in their best interests and serves to protect them from outraged citizens who might attack them at the polls. On one level, the episodes involving Old Man Gower and the hen with the yellow chicks are both retrospective (for Naomi as adult narrator) and prospective (for Naomi as child protagonist) parables of the country's failure in the role of parent, but with one significant difference. Unlike Old Man Gower and Mackenzie King, the hen, at least, was not a hypocrite.

Old Man Gower, however, is much more — and much more in Naomi's life — than a metonymic embodiment of Canada's misconduct. There is the matter of his misconduct, as well, which, although never specified, may have extended even to rape. For the text suggests more than Naomi consciously articulates. Thus she remembers how he would tell her not to tell her mother, and the resultant separation from her mother looms large in another memory: "In my childhood dreams," the chapter on Old Man Gower concludes, "the mountain yawns apart as the chasm spreads. My mother is on one side of the rift. I am on the other. We cannot reach each other. My legs are being sawn in half" (65). That last sentence does imply something more than loss of union with the mother, and may well be the child's subconscious rendering of a rape that cannot be consciously admitted or

43

acknowledged. Furthermore, the secret that separates her from her mother is not just the fact that, following Old Man Gower's directions, she does not tell. She fears that if she confides in her mother she will be "torn from her. But the secret has already separated us," she goes on to acknowledge, and "The secret is this: I go to seek Old Man Gower in his hideaway. I clamber unbidden onto his lap. His hands are frightening and pleasurable. In the center of my body is a rift" (64–65). This bodily rift, too, hints at rape, even as Naomi desperately denies abuse by claiming that she had consented to whatever was done to her.

The chick approaches the hen that attacks it; the child seeks out the man who abuses her. What do we make of such complicity? This is the question still riddling Naomi's account and asking, as she acknowledges at the beginning of this section of the novel just before she names Old Man Gower, "for answers still hidden from [her]" (61). One partial answer obviously is self-protection. Denial, in its various forms, can only go so far, and repression and even dissociation do not always save the personality under seige. If an assaulting force is too powerful to be resisted or denied, one sometimes identifies with that force, thereby allying the self with what would otherwise destroy it. That the consequences of similar assaults on the self (sexual abuse and racism) have been internalized is, in fact, suggested in the novel by Naomi's "dream of 'British' soldiers who forever rape anew, and beautiful Oriental women, naked and bound, whose 'only way to be saved from harm was to become seductive'" (Rose, "Hawthorne's 'Custom House'" 294).

Naomi's Patty Hearst-syndrome reaction is also seen on a more general level. The Japanese Canadians' persistent attempts to demonstrate good citizenship by accepting all that was done to them as "enemy aliens" is a version of coping through denial and identification rather similar to Naomi's complicity in her abuse. It is as if they both say "this isn't really happening, and even if it is I can change it through the way I accept it," and in each case such management of disaster best serves the interests of those who inflict it. Small wonder, then, that Naomi as an adult can occasionally denounce the stupidity of her people for how they responded to persecution — contributing, for example, to Fraser River flood relief to assist the very individuals who dispossessed them — but that mostly she insists the inevitable disasters of history are best buried in the past. In both cases, her

44

people's and her own, she rages inwardly at the victimization she can live with only by outwardly maintaining that for all practical purposes it amounts to nothing at all.

The psychic damage that Naomi suffers at the hands of Old Man Gower is further compounded by the fact that the metaphysical separation from the mother is soon followed by a physical separation. When, just a few months before the outbreak of the war, the mother leaves to return with her mother to Japan, Naomi, employing the projective thinking of a child, can hold herself responsible for that separation. She is being punished for her secret sin, and using the same childish prelogic, she thinks she is being further punished when the outbreak of the war brings the family still other losses in addition to that of the mother, whose absence continues. Also, and as with the actual abuse itself, Naomi never fully acknowledges the burden of her guilt, her pain, but again, too, the text hints at what the narrator is unable to recount. For example, she observes about her mother's impending departure, "I hardly dare to think, let alone ask, why she has to leave" (66), and we can well imagine what, under the circumstances, a five-year-old abused girl might think to ask herself regarding the why of that separation. Any such question also attests to how incongruously the burden on guilt falls on the victim and not on the victimizer, Old Man Gower. Bearing the blame and punishment for a crime not of her commission, Naomi here especially embodies the pattern of what will soon befall her people.

As the mother embarks for Japan, the traditional Japanese dockside farewell ceremony fails for Naomi. Those on the departing ship hold one end of a spooled streamer; those on the shore hold the other; and the unwinding paper ribbon symbolizes that they are still tied together and that this bond will not be broken by the journey when commencing. But Naomi does not know the meaning of the ceremony and cannot see her mother and grandmother "at the other end of a long paper streamer [that she clutches in her] fist" (66–67). In a real and prophetic sense, they are already lost to her, and all she has in their place are the streamers. She does, however, incorporate the central symbol of this parting ritual into her own private ceremony when, on returning home, she places a few of the unused streamer spools in one of her mother's sewing-machine drawers as "a surprise homecoming present for her" (67). A sign of leaving as a welcome-home gift! The imports ominously clash. She also includes two fluffy toy Easter chicks as part of the welcome-home present, and then, touchingly, pretends to be the mother returned home again to open the drawer and exclaim in happy surprise on discovering the gifts. But this enacted reunion of mother (Naomi) and daughter (the Easter chicks) necessarily recalls the disastrous failure of the union of the hen and the real chicks, and now there is no real mother present to make it all come right in the end.

Obasan soon moves into the house as a substitute for the missing mother, but her "warmth and constant presence" do not preclude an increasingly "ominous sense of cold and absence" (68–69). The children, for example, wake one night to utter darkness, which Stephen identifies as a blackout. They make their way towards the living room but are stopped by the sound of voices. The father and Old Man Gower are talking in the dark. This fact alone, for Naomi, is deeply disturbing. Old Man Gower has never been in their house before. Is she nowhere safe? But, even worse, it now seems that just as Obasan has supplanted the mother, this hypocritical disaster of a parental figure is in the process of replacing the father: "He seems more powerful than Father, larger and more at home even though this is our house" (69). There are other ominous hints of further victimization and impending dispossession. One day Stephen comes home beaten from school. Soon after, another student tells him — and he tells Naomi — that even the "Jap kids" are "bad" and they are all "going to be sent away" (70).

The nightmare way to that sending is portrayed in the novel from different but complementary perspectives. The simpler of the two is Naomi's memory of her confused and imperfect sense of what was happening during that troubled time. Thus she wonders whether the "Sick Bay" to which Grandfather Nakane has been sent is "near English Bay or Horseshoe Bay" (74). "The tension everywhere [that] was not clear to [her] then" (77) is experienced in more concrete terms when she recalls hiding under the cot where her father slept, planning to jump out to frighten him, but cowering there afraid to move when she heard groans and the sound of a fist pounding some surface. Similarly, when she "clamber[ed] onto [her father's] lap and put [her] arms around his neck" after the departure of Old Man Gower, she senses that "safety has not returned to him," and soon comes to suspect that "[t]he darkness is everywhere, in the day as well as the night," threatening them all "in all public places," falling "from the mouths of strangers," and sounding "in the taunts of children" (69–70).

Naomi, as a five-year-old child, did not fully understand the details of that darkness. She registered the existence of blackouts and curfews, lootings and confiscations, but not their fuller implications of freedoms curtailed and lives shattered. She came to know that Pool, like Sick Bay, was not another pleasant place on the ocean but was where people were held in preparation for being sent somewhere else. Fortunately, she never had to learn just how appalling that first place of confinement was: some 1,500 women as well as their children were assigned to camp — cramped and dehumanized — in the stalls of a livestock exposition building, stalls which were still crawling with maggots.

The larger perspective of a fuller and adult awareness that is also a passionate, immediate response to the unfolding tragedy of the time is to be found, not surprisingly, in Aunt Emily's packet. That discovery is also part of a basic narrative pattern in the novel. Wishing to escape painful old memories, Naomi shifts to the narrative present of 1972 and to such immediate matters as cleaning the house in preparation for Aunt Emily's and Stephen's arrival for Uncle's funeral. And still a captive of her own past, she does not put away the scattered items from Aunt Emily's package but picks up the large journal and begins to read. A deep ambivalence is also reflected in her first reaction to her aunt's diary/journal: "I feel like a burglar as I read, breaking into a private house only to discover it's my childhood house filled with corners and rooms I've never seen" (79). One of those corners, incidentally, is Naomi herself as a child as seen not through her own memories and retrospection, but through the perspective of her aunt as a young adult. The aunt recounts how the father once found Naomi repeatedly hitting her Japanese doll, and how she had cried long and inconsolably when he tried to take the doll from her, all of which definitely calls into question Naomi's claim that, as children, "[i]t happens to Stephen even more terrifyingly than it does to me" (70).

The journal is made up of copies of letters the aunt wrote to her older sister (Naomi's mother) in Japan. These letters, starting with the first, dated, ironically, 25 December 1941 (and contrasting the Christmas promise of the day with the brutal realities of the concluding year), comprise some 30 pages of the novel but they need not be summarized or assessed in detail. For the most part, Aunt Emily describes the unfolding hysteria of the time and the measures and actions it gave rise to — from the first ludicrous excesses, such as "a young Nisei boy with a metal lunch box" portrayed in the newspaper as "a spy with a radio transmitter" (85), to the final solution of the West Coast Japanese problem, the plan to remove permanently all those deemed Japanese from the "protected area."

SURVIVING THE WAR

Present and past oddly coalesce in the novel, partly because Naomi's persistent attempt to consign the past safely to the past has the paradoxical effect of keeping that past ever present, a hovering history waiting to claim again her attention and her narration. Thus, reading in Aunt Emily's journals and letters an account of the family's difficulties and uncertainties in the face of impending exile, she soon finds herself almost literally back on the train that carried her, Stephen, and Obasan away from Vancouver to the interior of British Columbia and the former ghost town of Slocan: "It is three decades ago and I am a small child resting my head in Obasan's lap" across from Stephen aboard a train "full of strangers" (112).

The narrative process whereby Naomi comes to be on the train again is almost as noteworthy as the social process that put her there in the first place, and comes right after the description of that process as set forth in Aunt Emily's journal. Indeed, the last entry in the journal details the further separation of the already war-divided family. Aunt Emily had arranged to be sent to Toronto. Obasan and the children were to leave the next day for Slocan. Aunt Emily records the details of rushed, last-minute preparation for different departures and of hasty goodbyes. Naomi, 30 years later, reads that final entry and remembers that "[t]he following day, May 22, 1942," she and her brother were with Obasan on the train to Slocan. "It is twelve years before [they] see Aunt Emily again" (110). That long absence means that the telling of subsequent events must now be turned over to Naomi herself. Her narration, however, will not be the straightforward chronology suggested by the phrase "the following day" in the penultimate sentence of chapter 14. Naomi's — and the novel's — return to the past is more complicated than that.

The next chapter begins: "I am sometimes not certain whether it is a cluttered attic in which I sit, a waiting room, a tunnel, a train. There is no beginning and no end to the forest, or the dust storm, no edge from which to know where the clearing begins" (111). That first sentence seemingly conjoins two actual pasts and two figurative relationships to the past/pasts. The first term of Naomi's possible metaphoric placement refers to her immediate narrative past — the cluttered attic she and Obasan just searched for the parcel from Aunt Emily that wasn't there. The fourth and final term, the train, is the one she rode 30 years earlier on the journey to Slocan that comes at the end of Aunt Emily's account of past tribulations, which Naomi has just read. And the two middle terms, the waiting room and the tunnel, suggest how Naomi, poised between two pasts, 30 years apart, doubly and differently confronts her different pasts. One can simply wait them out, consigning everything to the attic of memory and, even better, of forgetfulness. Or one can dig through one's past for meaning and significance, and perhaps even, as the second epigraph suggests, delve "down and down to the hidden voice" to "come at last to the freeing word." The passage, however, also denies the dichotomies it first seems to posit. As the "forest" of interior British Columbia slides into the "dust storm" of the Alberta prairie to give "no edge from which to know where the clearing [in forest or storm or memory or narrative] begins," we also see attic, waiting room, tunnel, and train merged into overlapping metaphors for a sense of the past.

Although Aunt Emily's parcel was not in the attic, other items awaited Naomi there, and they too served to transport (to tunnel?) her back to the past that always awaits her all the more irresistibly because, as noted, she is still waiting to come to terms with it. Moreover, she is presently waiting for other journeys to end, for Aunt Emily and Stephen to arrive, so that Uncle can be sent on his journey to death (a funeral as train and the grave as tunnel?). And on a still larger level, the passage evokes other questions crucial to Naomi: Into what cluttered attic did the country cast the Japanese, and how can it also cast aside that first casting? How has her mother so completely disappeared (which also turns out to be partly a matter of bureaucratic casting aside)? To where and to what did the trains take her? For the train that travels to the uncleared interior of the forest is succeeded not by a second train that takes her home to

Vancouver again, but by one that takes her still farther from home, to the beet fields and the dust storms of Alberta. Small wonder that Naomi is "not certain" of her placement, narratively speaking, or that one place or time can easily merge into another. In this sense, flashforwards are as much a feature of the narration as flashbacks, and the present time of the novel can be 1972, 1941, or any time in between. Indeed, Naomi's indefinite "I am *sometimes* not certain" spreads the "times" of her uncertainty over the whole range of chronological possibilities (111; emphasis added), and is itself an apt example of what P. Merivale has described as "memory . . . going in reverse" (79). Analogous to the Chinese poet Wang Wei and his dream of being a butterfly that might be dreaming of being a man, Naomi does not know if she is a present entity envisioning a past or a past one envisioning a present. Slips in time are the natural consequence of such uncertainty.

It is at this point, after briefly but cogently assessing Naomi's pervasive uncertainty and her consequent "longing" (for presence, for answers, for an emergence from as well as a different entry into "darkness"), and not after merely detailing the events, as recorded in Aunt Emily's journal, that lead up to that following day, 22 May 1942, that the novel makes such a slip:

1942.

We are leaving the B.C. coast — rain, cloud, mist — an air overladen with weeping. Behind us lies a salty sea within which swim our drowning specks of memory — our small waterlogged eulogies. We are going down to the middle of the earth with pick-axe eyes, tunnelling by train to the Interior, carried along by the momentum of the expulsion into the waiting wilderness. (111)

We note the present tense of the passage and we note too the way that present evokes the subsequent present that just evoked this previous one. Time, indeed, is "sometimes" (most times?) difficult to fix in this novel. Thus even in the ostensibly present tense of "1942" we can also be told that "[t]he memories are dream images," and then see those memories/dreams/images presented in explicit present-tense detail: "I am a small child resting my head in Obasan's lap. I am wearing a wine-coloured dirndl skirt with straps that criss-cross at the back. My white silk blouse has a Peter Pan collar dotted with tiny red flowers. I have a wine-coloured sweater with ivory duck buttons." Dressed in her best clothes for a journey to nowhere. How sad! "Kawaiso" (112, 113).

Others making the same journey more obviously elicit "kawaiso." That Japanese word, "used whenever there is hurt and a need for tenderness" (113), is voiced by Obasan at the sight of a frail and very young woman on the train carrying little else besides a "tiny red-faced baby" (112). Another woman on the train whispers that the young woman, Kuniko-san, was "rushed onto the train from Hastings Park, a few days after giving birth prematurely to her baby." Consequently, "[s]he has nothing. . . . [n]ot even diapers" (113). Obasan thereupon prepares a small gift package for the young mother, a towel and some apples and oranges, which she silently delivers with deep bows. The recipient bows in return. Then, in a scene that is one of the most moving in the entire novel and that merits quotation in its entirety, another gift is presented to the new baby and the new mother. An old woman sitting across from Naomi eases herself into the aisle:

"There is nothing to offer," she says as Obasan reaches her. She lifts her skirt and begins to remove a white flannel under-skirt, her hand gathering the undergarment in pleats.

"Ah, no no Grandmother," Obasan says.

"Last night it was washed. It is nothing, but it is clean."

Obasan supports her in the rock rock of the train and they sway together back and forth. The old woman steps out of the garment, being careful not to let it touch the floor.

"Please — if it is acceptable. For a diaper. There is nothing to offer," the old woman says as she hoists herself onto the seat again. She folds the undergarment into a neat square, the fingers of her hand stiff and curled as driftwood. Obasan bows, accept-ing the cloth, and returns to Kuniko-san and her baby, placing the piece of flannel on Kuniko-san's lap. Both their heads are bobbing like birds as they talk. Sometimes Kuniko-san bows so deeply, her baby touches her lap.

Leaning out into the aisle I can see better, and the old grand-mother nods, urging me to go to them. Kuniko-san is wiping her eyes in the baby's blanket. . . . (114)

The tears at the conclusion of this action are very different from the "air overladen with weeping," the image with which the journey began. They are the tears of sympathy and of sharing, the tears for things that move the human soul, and tears that totally refute the implicit assumption of the Canadian government that the Japanese Canadians on the deportation train were just so much chattel.

The interaction on the train places, in fact, any "inhuman" status precisely where it belongs. An inescapable contrast is that between the Canadian officials who "rushed" the new mother and her premature baby onto the train, neither providing her with any kind of layette nor allowing her time and opportunity to acquire a semblance of one of her own, and the two women who give what they can from the "nothing" that they were allowed to carry away after virtually everything had been seized or surrendered. Moreover, the hints here of a nativity scene (gifts for the baby born placeless, possessionless, practically on the road) also serve to suggest who the real upholders of basic Christian values were — not those Canadians who, certain of the rightness of their Western values, could consign others to exile, but the dispossessed, who were not at all dehumanized by their experience.

There are other significant contrasts and connections in this crucial scene. Naomi, for example, sees the new mother as "so young, I would call her 'o-nesan,' older sister" (113). *O-nesan* is the term Aunt Emily used, earlier in the journal, when referring to her older sister, Naomi's mother, who has already embarked upon a far longer journey into homelessness than the one Kuniko-san is here making. And just as Kuniko-san is a version of Naomi's mother, so, too, is Naomi a version of the baby on the train. Her wine-coloured sweater and skirt reflect the baby's "red-faced" guise, and create a colour echo that is given further substance by the consideration that *aka-chan*, "little red one," is the common informal Japanese word for *baby*. But Naomi is also a version of Kuniko-san, and not just because she is on the train with her favourite doll (as Kuniko-san is with her baby). She sees Kuniko-san hunched over the baby, her hair half-covering "her bird-like face" (113); then, as the gift is delivered, the young mother and Obasan are "bobbing like birds" (114). That double suggestion of Kuniko-san as a kind of bird recalls the episode of the killing of the yellow chicks as a parable of the treatment of the Japanese in Canada and foreshadows other episodes of birds figuring persecution (such as the young Japanese boys, in the camp at Slocan, torturing a chicken to death to prove that they still have power over something). Nor is Naomi herself exempt from that symbolism, as the duck buttons on her sweater attest.

Naomi emphasizes the transitory nature of the Japanese-Canadian settlement in the interior of British Columbia before giving any details about life in those settlements, and does so through another shift in time. Back in the narrative present of 1972, she describes how, 10 years earlier, Aunt Emily, on one of her trips west, decided that she wanted to visit the place where most of her family, along with many other Japanese Canadians, had spent most of the war. Aunt Emily, Uncle, Obasan, and Naomi take a trip through the mountains to the old ghost towns, to the work camps and the tar-paper-shack settlements erected almost overnight to receive the internees. What they encounter, however, is not what they came to see:

I drove through what was left of some of the ghost towns, filled and emptied once by prospectors, filled and emptied a second time by the Japanese Canadians. The first ghosts were still there, the miners, people of the woods, their white bones deep beneath the pine-needle floor, their flesh turned to earth, turned to air. Their buildings — hotels, abandoned mines, log cabins — still stood marking their stay. But what of the second wave? What remains of our time there? (117)

All signs of the Japanese presence — the huts, the camps — have been removed, as if these people and their ordeal never were, so that even the ghosts of this place can seem an unsullied white again. Yet the landscape is not completely unmarked. As Naomi notes, "[t]he mountains too were unchanged except for the evidence of new roads and a larger logging industry." And, "[n]ow, down on the shore of the Slocan lake, on the most beautiful part of the sandy beach, where we used to swim, there was a large new sawmill owned by someone who lived in New York" (117, 118). Those different but not unrelated scars attest that the country is still destroying parts of itself.

As the retrospective recounting of the return visit to Slocan slides into the present-tense account of the exiled Japanese arriving and settling there, we see one major reason why few signs of that settlement remained 20 years later. The accommodations provided were, figuratively, already on their last legs. Thus the house in which Naomi was going to live is first remembered (past tense) as "just a two-roomed log hut" that "was shabby and sagging and overgrown with weeds when we first saw it on that spring day in 1942" (118), and is then seen (present tense) by the six-year-old Naomi in more graphic detail:

> We walk a few steps farther down the path, and there, almost hidden from sight off the path, is a small grey hut with a broken porch camouflaged by shrubbery and trees. The colour of the house is that of sand and earth. It seems more like a giant toadstool than a building. The mortar between the logs is crumbling and the porch roof dives down in the middle. A "V" for victory. From the road, the house is invisible, and the path to it is overgrown with weeds. (120–21)

The inside is no better. The two rooms are low and cramped, musty and grey; the walls are partly covered with peeling newspaper; the cracks caulked with grass and cow manure.

The decaying house is only one sign of the family's fallen fortunes. On the way to the house is "a wooden bridge over a creek." As she crosses that bridge, Naomi

> think[s] of the curved bridge over the goldfish pond at Obasan's house, and the bridges Stephen and [she] made in the sand to the desolate sound of the sea, and the huge Lions' Gate Bridge in Stanley Park, and the terrifying Capilano swinging bridge that trembled as we crossed it high up in the dangerous air. (119–20)

From all that to this! Kogawa also has Naomi first note that "while standing on [the Slocan] bridge," she loses her favourite doll, and consequently often "feel[s] a certain sadness" crossing that same bridge (120). The lost doll here reflects the lost mother. The bridge crosses a stream that makes its way down to the ocean (the lost ocean to which Naomi cannot, for years, return, and from the other side of which her mother will never return) and thus evokes "the stream [of the poetic epigraph] down and down to the hidden voice" that Naomi, for a long time, cannot follow to its mouth. Moreover, the loss of the doll is soon followed by another, greater loss, which is also poetically linked to the bridge and the stream:

It is twilight, and Obasan and I are standing on the bridge watching a large school of tiny fish shimmering upstream like a wriggling grey cloud. We are on our way to the wake in the Odd Fellows Hall. It is all so strange. Grandma Nakane, Obasan tells me, is in heaven. (127)

Kogawa does not rely on such traditional tools of the novelist as a carefully deployed and structured plot or characters enmeshed in that plot and developed in terms of it. Instead, she writes mostly as if the novel were part personal memoir and part historical reportage, but a memoir/history as recounted by a lyric poet attuned to resonant details and patterns of recurrent images and verbal echoes. Thus, in the passage just quoted, we encounter again the twilight/night, bridge/stream, and death/silence tropes that interweave throughout the novel starting with the epigraphs and the first episode. Or, in a different register, we can notice the comic incongruity of the site of the funeral. How odd it would be to the original Odd Fellows who built the hall to see it now used for a Japanese/Canadian Christian/Buddhist funeral! But that incongruous consequence of forced relocation is itself overshadowed by more poetic evocations of final journeys and transformations. The "grey cloud" of "fish shimmering upstream" anticipates the cremation of the grandmother's body on the mountainside the following day.

At their best, Kogawa's poetic effects, like all good poetry, cannot be reduced to paraphrase and explication. For example, when Naomi first sees the house she will live in and describes it as being the colour of "sand and earth," as looking "more like a giant toadstool than a building," we note the way colour almost predicts a collapse, one that seems all the more imminent because of the house's mushroom qualities. These qualities, incidentally, seem more those of a toadstool (a poisonous mushroom) than a *matsutake* (a mountain mushroom that also grows in the Slocan area and that is prized in Japanese cuisine[9]). Although these poetic details can be largely translated into critical prose, the original is certainly more evocative and effective than the expostulation. And other effects are for the most part beyond explanation. When the children first enter the house they hear the older people trying to make the best of its depressing condition. "Short people lived here, the same as we are," comments the old man who carried the family's possessions from the train on his homemade wheelbarrow. Nakayama-sensei, the family's minister, the man who guided them to their "new" quarters, offers a prayer of thanks: "For our life and that we are together again, thank you. For protection thus far, thank you . . ." (122). During that prayer, to escape the cribbed and confined false comfort it seems to represent (What "protection"? Why "together"? Father, Mother, Uncle, Aunt Emily, and all four grandparents are all somewhere else), the children make their escape through a rusty, screened back door into "[t]he green air once more," where they encounter a descending flight of butterflies:

> As we stand here looking over an overgrown tangle of weeds and vines, the air is suddenly swarming with butterflies. Up and down like drunken dancers, the gold and brown winged things come down the side of the mountain fluttering awkwardly. There are dozens of them. Some park like tiny helicopters on grass stalks, flexing their wings as if for take-off. Others hover near the ground before spilling back up into the air, ungainly as baby ballerinas. They are all dressed in the same velvet brown. (122)

Is this an image of hope? It is hard to say. The beauty of the scene partly suggests that nature is a peaceful refuge from, or at least an alternative to, the problems humans are heir to, yet the butterflies flutter "awkwardly," "like drunken dancers," and park mechanically, like "tiny helicopters," as if they were entering our world instead of allowing us some access to theirs. The odd simile, "ungainly as baby ballerinas," also implies that butterflies and children are both out of place and limited to being less than they might be. To further emphasize this possible equivalence, Kogawa then describes Stephen embarking on a grotesque and awkward dance of his own, a dance of death. He begins slashing at the butterflies, "hopping deeper and deeper into the tall grasses, swinging his crutch like a scythe" (123). Stephen as the Grim Reaper? Of butterflies? The action is partly explained by Stephen himself: " 'They're bad,' [he] says as he wades through the weeds. 'They eat holes in your clothes' " (123). Obviously, Stephen wants to claim and exercise the same power of definition and disposal that the country has claimed with respect to Japanese Canadians, and just as obviously he is equally wrong in his assessment of "vermin." This action concludes when he "reaches the end of the yard [and] turns around. Some brambles and vines are clinging to his pant leg and one butterfly he cannot see is hovering above his head" (123). Entangled in more than brambles and vines, Stephen is almost redeemed by that one uncanny presence far harder to read than the original swarm. Significance might be here best rendered in koan: Do butterflies have Buddha nature? Or in haiku: A lone butterfly, / After the long massacre, / Hovers in the sky.

Kogawa can pass rather quickly over Naomi's three years in Slocan partly because the author's poetics of dispossession have already rendered a detailed recounting of the protagonist's deprivations largely superfluous. Furthermore, because this portion of the novel is narrated in the present tense, it must reflect Naomi's limited childhood perspective on what is happening to her and her family rather than her retrospective adult awareness of the gross injustice of it all. Thus Naomi can fumble towards some understanding of her grandmother's death — "Can Grandma Nakane see us from heaven, I wonder. Could her spirit be in the little grey fishes?" (127) — and hardly notice the incongruous presence of another grandmother figure standing in for the real one, who is kept from them by, first, bureaucratic fiat; then, illness; and, finally, death. Nomura-obasan, the unrelated, almost bedridden old woman who lives for the first few years with Naomi, Stephen, Obasan, and then Uncle, too (after he is allowed to come back from the labour camp), in their two-room shack, also testifies to how poorly accommodated the Japanese Canadians were during their Slocan exile as well as to how much they accommodated each other.

The innocent, inexperienced child narrating what happens at Slocan is not, however, exactly the same Naomi who, as a child, endured those same events. This is another reason for the regular chronological slippage of the novel; the adult narrator cannot cast herself back into the child she was in 1942, 1943, 1944, but only into the child she can remember or reconstruct from her present vantage point. At a few places this double perspective is explicitly signalled in the text. Once, for example, when the required bedpan could not immediately be found, Naomi helps Nomura-obasan to the outhouse. Back in her bed again, the old woman "sighs contentedly and listens to the nasal-voiced man on the record singing 'Darling, I am growing old, Silver threads among the gold. . . .'" As Stephen plays

one of the missing mother's favourite records, the song's romanticiz-
ing of age is played out against Nomura-obasan's slow and painful
trip to the outhouse. More to the point, the song's implicit promise
of marriage, family, and stability only emphasizes, for both Stephen
and Naomi, that the father and the mother are no longer a central
and centring couple whose love can hold at bay the vicissitudes of
time. Instead of growing old together, they are permanently parted
and on their different ways to different lonely deaths brought on by
something more than beautiful aging. Beauty and aging are, moreover, both coded white. As Naomi notes: "It does not occur to me
to wonder why mother would have liked this song. We do not have
silver threads among the gold" (126). And that is the final ironic
incongruity of this episode. The six-year-old Naomi tells us what, as
a six-year-old, she did not think to think.

More typically, however, Naomi, in the Slocan sections of *Obasan*,
serves as a limited narrator who reports events replete with implications beyond her childhood ken, implications provided by the
author's structuring of the narrative and of what her protagonist
thereby recounts. Naomi can, for example, graphically tell how her
life was saved yet leave to the reader the large task of working out
the structural implications of that crucial episode and the complex
ways in which it addresses the question of discrimination. For Naomi
nearly drowns shortly after she and two other playmates toss an
insect on a stick into a stream and watch it "clinging tenaciously" as
it "rushes headlong downstream" to be caught in an eddy where they
"abandon it . . . bobbing and dancing in its whirlpool" (140). The
whirlpool suggests the vortex of history in which Japanese Canadians have been caught, a vortex that has left many of them stranded,
abandoned in Slocan, just as the insect on the stick represents,
generally, those people who cling tenaciously to their claims that they
are Canadian citizens who do not at all deserve to be cast aside. More
specifically, as we soon see, the insect also anticipates Naomi herself
on a raft drifting towards her own brush with death.

The misadventure of a red insect provides an outer frame for the
near drowning, which is further framed with a narrative about the
First People, the "Redskins," provided by Rough Lock Bill, a "scrag-
gly" and "knobbly" character whom Naomi and Kenji (the boy who
threw the insect into the stream) encounter a week later while playing
on the shore of Lake Slocan (144). Despite his disreputable appear-

ance, this older man falls into an immediate, easy camaraderie with the children, asking Naomi her name, having her write it with his stick in the wet sand when she is too shy to say it aloud, writing his own name for her to read. Then, scooping out, in the sandy shore, a miniature version of the large mountain lake and piling up small pyramids of sand to represent the surrounding peaks, he engraves *Slocan*, too, in the sand, and asks them if they "[w]anna hear a story" of the place. It is a story that comes with both prologue and protocols:

> Rough Lock cleans off a brome grass tree and shoves it in between two teeth at the side of his mouth. As he talks, the grass moves back and forth like a flag. "Never met a kid didn't like stories. Red skin, yellow skin, white skin, any skin." He puts his brown leathery arm beside Kenji's pale one. "Don't make sense, do it, all this fuss about skin?"
> "Nope," he says when we don't answer. "It sure don't, Rough Lock." (145)

The asserted universality of story implicitly subsumes and erases smaller narratives of difference and discrimination, whether based on age, gender, or race — and notice that the white Rough Lock is darker than the coloured Kenji. Yet the particular story that is going to do this important and ongoing work is itself mostly written, literally and figuratively, in the sand. Rough Lock Bill's obviously marginal status serves, too, to undercut the centrality of his story, even as that marginality also situates him, literally and figuratively, at his story's centre:

> "You from Vancouver?"
> I nod.
> "Big city." He shakes his head. "All that cement ["see-ment," he says] addles the brain."
> He jabs his finger in the sand. "This here's the best place there is." (145)

The "where" of an ostensibly central "here," always problematic in Canadian narration — becomes even more so as the tale unfolds. Told also partly in the sand, it derives from a "[l]ong time ago" when only Native people lived in the area and when many of them were dying:

"Don't know what it was. Smallpox maybe. Tribe wars. Starvation. Maybe it was a hex, who knows? But there's always a few left when something like that happens. And this brave, he set out to find a place. A good place with lots of good food — deer, fish, berries. Know where that was?"

"Where?" Kenji asks.

"Well, I tell ya, it took him a long time to get here. But he knew it when he saw it. This right here. Right here." He waves his arm indicating the lake and the beach. "So he goes all the way back to where his people are, back past these mountains, and he says to them, 'If you go slow, you can go.' So off we go, these few here, some so weak they have to be carried. Took all of them together — how long? Months? A year? 'If you go slow,' he says, 'you can go. Slow can go. Slow can go.' Like a train chugging across the mountains."

Kenji is helping him march the stick people around and around the mountains till they come to the edge of the sand-hole lake. "We call it Slocan now. Real name is Slow-can-go." (145–46)

On one level this is a story of cooperative survival and of a patient endurance of adversity that is very Japanese, and thus evokes the Japanese Canadians who have most recently followed in the footsteps of those first inhabitants. This tale of precontact times is also obviously haunted by the ghost of white people to come (with their smallpox and trains), so it is not surprising that the story of how the original inhabitants came to the great good place concludes with none of them still in residence. " 'When my Grandad came, there was a whole tribe here.' He points a stick at his cabin. 'Right there was the chief's tepee. But last I saw — one old guy up past the mine — be dead now probably' " (146). In the chief's place, though he is hardly the chief, Rough Lock Bill has told a story of the real name that cannot be the real name but must be only an English approximation of the missing Native original. The story of the Native people coming into possession of the place similarly evokes the story of how they subsequently lost it to others, as well as the even later story of still others being exiled to it after the first successors had mostly left. These different stories inscribe again the very significance of the "fuss about skin" — "[r]ed skin, yellow skin, white skin" — that their narrator originally discounted.

Vaguely discontent with his tale — "smart people don't talk too much. Redskins know that" (147) — Rough Lock leaves the children, who go back to their play. Naomi and Kenji now venture out on the log raft Kenji had previously found. He poles out to deeper water, slips, and falls in, and then flounders to shore while she slowly floats farther out onto the lake. She ignores his cries to jump because, as she shouts back, she cannot swim. When Kenji "turns suddenly and flees" from the scene, she decides she has been abandoned to her own devices and must save herself before it is too late: "Farther out the lake goes on forever. I will be utterly lost. Perhaps I can swim. I have watched the others. I must leap now, without hesitating, before I drift farther" (148). She jumps and is about to drown, but since Kenji has actually run to seek help, Rough Lock Bill arrives in time to pull her, "as through a wavering tunnel" and "slow as a courtly dance" (149), from the water. The tunnel looks back to the poetic epigraph and the way "down and down to the hidden voice." The dance looks forward to the loss she later envisions her mother acknowledging through dance. In short, she almost joins in death her mother who has not yet died. But there is a still larger resonance in this action. Rough Lock Bill counterbalances Old Man Gower. The one older white man figuratively destroyed her life; the other, later, literally saves it. The story Rough Lock Bill tells does not finally refute discrimination, but his role in Naomi's story (which includes telling her his) does.

Not all white Canadians, Kogawa is careful to show, were complicit in the official racism of the time. Neither were all Japanese Canadians simply the innocent victims of such discrimination, for they could do unto themselves much as they were done by, as another episode later in the account of the internment at Slocan demonstrates. One evening Naomi and Obasan are "removing the tiny round black dots, hard as BB shot" (161), from some recently purchased rice. They spread the adulterated rice out on a tray and swiftly flick aside any bits of foreign matter. Purifying the rice as an analogue to purifying the race? That problematic imagistic equation is further suggested by subsequent events. Uncle returns from his bath and reminds them they still have not had theirs. When, later than ever before, they finally enter the bathhouse, Naomi sees that she and Obasan have been, themselves, figuratively cast aside. Two of the three older women still present do not greet the new arrivals at all; a couple of Naomi's lingering playmates are called from the water and hurried on their way. Never, Naomi notices, has this place, which is "always filled with a slow steamy chatter from women and girls" (160), been "so empty of banter"; "never" has she "felt the edges" of disapproval she experiences there this night (163).

Only later does Naomi find out what Obasan apparently already knew and wanted to spare her niece from knowing by bathing so late. Returning home, she trails behind her aunt and encounters again the two girls who were called away at the bath. One still wants to be Naomi's friend, but the other insists: " 'My mom says we can't play with you.' . . . 'You're sick. You've all got TB. You and the Nomuras and your dad.' Her words are spraying out in a rush and she points her finger at me. 'That's why Stephen is limping' " (165). Naomi is excluded not just because of the ascribed disease, but also because of its postulated causes and consequences. "You sleep on the floor! . . . That's how you get it." And because you have it, "[n]obody will marry you" (166). This condemning of Naomi demonstrates, as does an earlier scene in which Japanese-Canadian boys torture a chicken to death, that the victims need their victims too.

What seems a simple matter of black and white with the rice (and I say "seems" because, as Mary Douglas cogently argues in *Purity and Danger*, the "natural" distinction between the natural and the contaminant is always culturally constructed) becomes more complicated when we move from sustenance to people. Canadians of European ancestry claim native status, but then deny that same status to immigrants from elsewhere as well as to the country's aboriginal inhabitants. These contradictions are effectively foregrounded in the novel when the Japanese-Canadian students rush from the killing of the chicken to the start of a new school day and the singing of the national anthem. The ironies are palpable, beginning with the anthem's first lines and the proclaimed patriot love that some native sons and daughters have been commanded not to show:

O Canada, our home and native land
True patriot love in all thy sons command
With glowing hearts we see thee rise
The true north strong and free. . . .

And as the singing ends — "*O Canada, glorious and free / O Canada, we stand on guard for thee!*" (156) — one must wonder if keeping

Japanese Canadians in work crews, resettlement camps, and prisons (for those who declined the crews and the camps) was quite the "standing on guard" the author of these words had in mind. Suffice to say that this particular voicing of the national anthem becomes chiefly a lament for a country that can maintain such camps.

Caught in the contradictions of "native" and "land," "patriot" and "command," Japanese Canadians predictably enact their own ceremonies of exclusion and affiliation, starting with an internalization of the dubious standards whereby they are condemned and an acting out of the consequent self-hatred. "Not that kind of food" (115), Stephen says when Obasan offers him a rice ball on the train to Slocan. He wants "real" food, and later she does her best, sending him to school with peanut-butter sandwiches and a thermos of hot soup, in contrast to Naomi's "two moist and sticky rice balls with a salty red plum in the center of each, a boiled egg to the side with a tight square of lightly boiled greens" (153).

The immigrant's conundrum: In the context of a different culture, what is the essential "rice"; what is the intruding "foreign matter"; and how can I, poised between the old unapplicable and the new unknown, be always right in those difficult decisions and avoid being designated "foreign matter" myself? That ongoing crisis of uncertain identity underlies the charge of "TB" directed at Naomi and, even more, the underlying "logic" of the charge — that you get it by sleeping on the floor, which is, after all, where Japanese traditionally sleep but where Naomi, we have been specifically told, does not. Nevertheless, in an odd combination of projection and denial, scapegoating and self-hatred, her friend implies that if they were all Canadian enough, she would not be sick (even though she is not) and they would not be there (even though they would). The accusation seems even odder when we notice that it is delivered as they all return from the quintessentially Japanese communal bathhouse.

The bathhouse also signifies the way the Japanese Canadians, although consigned to ghost towns and hastily constructed camps, struggle to make a bearable life for themselves. At the bath they can be, mostly, "one flesh, one family, washing each other or submerged in the hot water, half awake, half asleep" (160–61), at peace with themselves and the world. Building the bathhouse is part, too, of a general rebuilding of Slocan. "The ghost town is alive and kicking like Ezekiel's resurrected valley of bones," and some of "them bones" are "jitterbugging in the Odd Fellows Hall" or "skating in the rinks" or "running up and down the mountainsides and the streets and paths of Slocan" (160). And as "the community flourishes with stores, crafts, gardens, and [such] home-grown enterprise[s]" as Sakamoto Tailors, Nose Shoe Hospital, Tahara's Barber Shop, Tokyo Sobaya, Tak Toyota's photo studio, Shigeta watch repair, and Kasubuchi dressmaker (160), it becomes as much a Japantown as was the Powell Street area in Vancouver, which had been known as Nihon-machi (Japantown). It can be assumed that the authorities will be no more pleased with this second Japantown than they were with the first. Not surprisingly, then, the end of the war will not bring for the internally exiled internees a return to normal life, but a second exile and a diaspora more devastating than the first.

SURVIVING THE PEACE

For Naomi the first implication of the end of the war is particularly perturbing. She partly awakens one morning, "suddenly, before the regular summons of the rooster," because "[s]omething has touched [her]" (167). That something — "not human, not animal" — is soon recognized as the preternatural presence of her mother: "She is here. She is not here. She is reaching out to me with a touch deceptive as down, with hands and fingers that wave like grass around my feet, and her hair falls and falls and falls from her head like streamers of paper rain." That last detail explicitly evokes Naomi's original separation from her mother, who, indeed, is next sensed as "a ship leaving the harbour, tied to me by coloured paper streamers that break and fall into a swirling wake" — a wake that threatens to wash away Naomi even as she fully awakens from this disturbing dream/vision (167). But the hair falling like paper streamers also implicitly invokes the reason why that first parting became permanent. As the novel makes clear, the mother here "appears" immediately after the conclusion of the war. The previous day Stephen had come running home shouting "[w]e won, we won, we won" (168), and had nailed a Union Jack flag to the roof of the house to celebrate that victory. We, as readers, know, while Stephen and Naomi do not, that Japan unconditionally surrendered after the second atomic bomb was dropped on Nagasaki. In this context, hair falling like "streamers of paper rain" inescapably suggests radiation sickness, and thus the compound metaphor conjoins the sign of an ostensibly temporary separation (the paper streamers) with the sign that it now will be permanent (the falling hair). No wonder Naomi is confused and knows "[s]omething is happening" but not "what it is" (167). Only near the end of the novel, when she is finally told that her mother was in Nagasaki in the summer of 1945 and not, as believed, in Tokyo, can she finally understand who came to her and how and why.

When Naomi arises to escape this visitation of the mother, she finds that the father, in a more real sense, has returned as well. Boxes, she notices, are piled everywhere in Uncle and Obasan's room; the furniture has been rearranged; someone is stretched out on a cot that was not there before. Recognizing who it is, she flings herself onto the cot and into his embrace. In contrast to "the nightmare . . . as persistent as rain" that she has just endured (169), his presence is totally reassuring: "I am Goldilocks, I am Momotaro returning. I am leaf in the wind restored to its branch, child of my father come home. The world is safe once more and Chicken Little is wrong. The sky is not falling down after all" (170). She even imagines herself falling, but falling like that restored leaf, "safe as a feather," back from Slocan through reversed train and bus rides to "our house and the hedge around the yard and the peach tree outside my window and the goldfish bowl in the music room" (170).

Unfortunately, her immediately subsequent fall will be in quite another direction, as is suggested by several loaded details of this second reunion scene. For example, Naomi's fairy-tale reference to being Goldilocks (that is, valued and saved), overlooks the fact that she isn't, and that her dark hair still has a different significance than Goldilocks's yellow tresses. This consideration is emphasized in the text by one of her first actions on awakening that same morning. A trusted teacher had told Stephen that black hairs left in water would turn into water snakes. He has set up a "watersnake bowl," which Naomi checks to see if the anticipated transformation has occurred (169). The hairs have not changed — neither into snakes, nor, for that matter, into strands of gold. The Japanese fairy-tale reference is not particularly promising either. Although Momotaro suggests Naomi's old home, and particularly the peach tree just outside her window, he is, after all and as earlier noted, a protagonist without real parents and one who leaves his substitute home and family. But most telling are the repeated crows of the rooster. The chapter describing the reappearances of both Naomi's parents begins with this creature's "choked chirp" (167), and the joyous reunion with the father is framed by the double observation (before and after) that "outside the rooster is still crowing" (170). The rooster is, significantly, a bantam, a Chicken Little whose cry is heard but not attended. In a very real sense the sky is still falling.

Naomi soon sees in her "Father's eyes" that "[i]t's happening again, it's happening again" (172). "It" is another exile, another relocation. The fact that the war has ended does not mean that they can go home. Instead, the home established after the first exile is to be broken up again, just as the family is finally being partly reunited in it. Japanese Canadians will again be dispossessed and dispersed. Again, too, they are caught in an impossible double bind: they are required either to acknowledge their disloyalty by agreeing to repatriation or to demonstrate it by resisting the program set up to return them to Japan. Once more, difference is invoked and used to justify government control. Something must still be done about the "Japanese problem." Those who "want" to return must be separated from those who decline to accept the government's final solution to the problem of their presence, and this second group is, in turn, further subdivided into those designated for eastern placement (dispersal throughout the provinces east of British Columbia) and those not deemed suitable for such placement. Each category has its assigned relocation camps. Uncle receives a letter consigning him to one category and one camp. The father goes into another category and to a different camp. His letter of consignment, which Naomi reads 27 years later when she receives Aunt Emily's packet, "is imperative and must be obeyed" (173). Again, there are hasty, fearful removals, sad farewells, and confusion and loss: "suddenly Father is not here again and [Naomi does] not know what is happening" (179). Presently, she is leaving Slocan too. On a train, "exactly like the last time" (180), she travels not back to Vancouver and home, but into another exile.

Their exile from exile takes Naomi, Stephen, Obasan, and Uncle to a one-room dirt-floor hut on the edge of a sugar-beet field in Alberta. At this veritable (at least so it seems) "edge of the world" (191), the ordered Japanese community life that had been established in Slocan is superseded by a lonely existence of hardship and toil. As

66

Ken Adachi observes in *The Enemy That Never Was*, "[p]erhaps no other group of evacuees had to suffer as much harrowing deprivation and hardship" as those sent to southern Alberta to work for farmers who mostly "looked upon [them] as a ready source of slave or prisoner-of-war labour, ripe for exploitation, which, under the terms of the agreement with the province" they indeed were (281).

For Naomi, this second new life, even in retrospect, is a nightmare "from which there is no waking." But even though she "cannot bear the memory" of what she went through (194), she still must attest to that experience. In contradistinction to the official representation, to the newspaper photo of Japanese workers captioned "Grinning and Happy" that is part of Aunt Emily's packet (193), Naomi enumerates the things she minded, which is pretty much everything. She hated the "chicken coop 'house' " in which they baked in July and froze in January, the flies that in summer would "curtain the windows" (194), the bedbugs that would sometimes force her to sleep on the table; "the muddy water from the irrigation ditch," which they drank after boiling and straining, but still with "tiny carcasses of water creatures at the bottom of the cup" (195).

But worst was the work "in the beet field under the maddening sun," and "lying down in the ditch, faint, and the nausea in waves and the cold sweat, and getting up and tackling the next row" and doing so "day after day and not even wondering how this has come about" (195). Nor is it just the work that weighs Naomi down. The "sleep-walk years" of her "growing-up days" are a time of "sadness" and "absence . . . like a long winter storm" because both her parents are missing (200). The end of the war did not bring the mother back, but took the father away again, and his absence, too, becomes painfully permanent. A few letters arrive from him. The first informs the family that Grandfather Nakane "died of a heart attack the day before [they] left Slocan," thus conjoining departure and death. The last, received, ironically, "around Christmas, 1949, [and telling] something about a doctor [the father] doesn't trust," presages the father's own death, which occurs the following spring after an unsuccessful operation (200).

The father's death is foreshadowed another way, too. On spring evenings Naomi would sometimes visit a nearby swamp as an escape from the world of perpetual labour that otherwise constitutes her life. During one such visit she finds a frog with a broken leg. She

67

decides to keep it and to make a safe home for it in a glass bowl. The frog as a small creature in need of a haven — of a substitute home — certainly reflects Naomi herself, just as its particular injury recalls Stephen on his crutches. But for Naomi the frog especially represents her father. She decides to call it Tad, short for both Tadpole and Tadashi, her father's first name, and she imagines it coming "from the mountains," "a messenger from my father" (206). When she returns home, however, there is another messenger. Nakayama-sensei, after a particularly long absence, is paying an obviously portentous visit, the significance of which Naomi may have read as she entered the room: "I am not sure, as I remember the scene, whether I am told after I come in, or later at night when I am in bed, or if I am even told at all. It's possible the words are never said outright. I know that for years I simply do not believe it" (206). The last "it" — a pronoun conspicuously missing any clarifying anteced-ent — is the father's death, which is also hinted at when the frog's subsequent disappearance is juxtaposed with the observation that "[m]y last letter to Father has received no answer" (208).

Only later does Naomi discover the parallels between the loss of her father and the loss of the mother. One parent was taken from her and the other kept from her by bureaucratic fiat, and both separations became final at approximately the same time. Aunt Emily's file contains the answers to her applications for the readmission to Canada of Naomi's mother and grandmother. Naomi reads, 12 years later, the baldly stated reasons both are refused. Grandma Kato, by returning to Japan, "relinquished any claim to Canadian domicile which she might previously have acquired" and, as a Japanese national, is "not admissible under existing regulations," so "no encouragement can be offered" in her case (212–13). Naomi's moth-er's situation is somewhat different in that she is a Canadian citizen. However, her application for readmission also requested that her four-year-old niece and adopted daughter be allowed to accompany her. This is the sticking point. The child is inadmissible, of course, which also conveniently allows for keeping the mother out:

It is regretted that the Department is unable to extend any facilities for admission of the child at the present time. It is assumed that Mrs. Nakane would not desire to come forward alone, leaving the child in Japan, and therefore it can only be suggested that the matter of her return be left in abeyance until such time in the future as there may be a change in the regulations respecting admission of Japanese nationals which would enable the Department to deal with the application of the child. (213)

This official reluctance to be party to any separation of mother and child is flagrantly hypocritical. Why not simply admit them both? Moreover, this mother's real children, Stephen and Naomi, are, like their mother, also Canadian citizens and they reside in Canada. Yet she is to be kept from them by a racist policy that the government tries to pass off as a humanitarian acknowledgement of the sacred bond of motherhood.

Reading these "puzzling letter[s]," Naomi also remembers another "puzzling incident" pertaining to her mother (213). Some four years after the applications for readmission were refused, Aunt Emily made her first visit from Toronto. She stayed for a week, a week Naomi mostly spent studying for the senior matriculation exams she was about to take. On the last night of her aunt's visit Naomi had gone to sleep over "an unresolved algebra equation" (219). A few hours later she awakened to hear snippets of a perturbing conversation: " 'Kodomo no tame.' . . . For the sake of the children. . . . 'But they are not children. They should be told' " (219). This, too, was a kind of unresolved algebra equation. If the children who should not be told are no longer children, then what is it they should not be told? Naomi did not then ascertain the answer even though she saw Obasan (as she had at other difficult times, such as after the death of the father) praying and Aunt Emily crying.

Naomi, in 1954, overheard a conversation she was not supposed to hear regarding something she was not supposed to be told, and witnessed Aunt Emily, at the end of this discussion, placing a few blue papers in a grey cardboard folder, closing it, and putting it away. Eighteen years and one chapter later, the same "grey cardboard folder [is there] in Aunt Emily's package," and so are the same folded sheets of blue paper (221). Here is the solution to the earlier problem of what the children were not to be told, which also explains the larger question of why the mother never returned. The answers herein contained, however, are still hidden from Naomi because, although she speaks Japanese, she cannot read the Japanese writing, "like a bead curtain of asterisks" (234), on these portentous pages. Obasan, however, can, and she does so, in a slow and tortuous fashion, following "each line down" and then starting "again at the top of the next row" like "a beet worker hoeing . . . a beet field" (221), while she and Naomi wait for the arrival of Stephen and Aunt Emily from Toronto.

The waiting is interrupted by the arrival of Mr. and Mrs. Barker, the family's former employers and landlords, who come to offer their condolences; to ask — in Pidgin English — if Obasan can "[m]anage all right" after the death of Uncle (225); and to recommend the merits of Sunnydale Lodge, the local "white-walled white-washed, and totally white old folks' home," where "Obasan would be as welcome," Naomi knows, "as a Zulu warrior" (224). Naomi also knows that this show of concern, this demonstration of the desire to do the right thing, is both too little and too late. She notices that Mr. Barker invites himself and his wife — " 'Come in, Vivian,' he urges her" (222) — into Obasan's house and recalls that, years earlier, when invited by the Barker's daughter to their house, the door was slammed in her face. Also, when Mr. Barker praises Uncle as someone who "[n]ever once said a bitter word" (225), his commendation is rather compromised by the consideration that any such bitter word — a complaint about the long hours in the beet fields, say, or about the chicken-coop hut — could well have been directed towards him. "It was a terrible business what we did to our Japanese," Mr. Barker continues, as if acknowledgement of injury constitutes restitution. What Naomi registers is further injury:

"Ah, here we go again," she muses. "Our Indians." "Our Japanese." "A terrible business." It's like being offered a pair of crutches while I'm striding down the street. The comments are so incessant and always so well-intentioned. "How long have you been in this country? Do you like our country? You speak such good English. Do you run a café?"

Such comments are, for Naomi, offensively patronizing. They are "icebreaker questions that create an awareness of ice" by reminding her of her presumed outcast status, by showing her that she is not seen as someone who is as Canadian as any other resident or citizen (225). She immediately counters: "Oh Canada, whether it is admitted or not, we come from you we come from you. From the same soil,

70

the slugs and slime and bogs and twigs and roots. We come from the country that plucks its people out like weeds and flings them into the roadside." And, she continues, with reference to the poetic epigraph and previous (and future) dreams, "[w]e come from cemeteries full of skeletons with wild roses in their grinning teeth. We come from our untold tales that wait for their telling." But, most of all, "[w]e come from Canada, this land that is like every land, filled with the wise, the fearful, the compassionate, the corrupt" (226). In this powerful and passionate proclamation of collective identity, Naomi's "we" is obviously very different from Mr. Barker's in his "what we did to our Japanese." Nevertheless, in seeing Canada as an everyland filled with both the good and the bad, Naomi sounds a theme of forgiveness and broad human awareness that soon becomes more prominent. Mr. Barker's present concern, albeit tinged with patron-ization, is preferable to his previous exploitation of his tenants, which was itself more his government's doing than his own.

As someone who has lived several years in Japan, I know that the questions regularly asked the foreigner — Do you like rice? Can you use chopsticks? — are almost as annoying as those that bothered Naomi. But while in Japan, I was also fortunate enough to teach *Obasan* to a group of alumnae of the college where I was a visiting professor. I expected that the older members of this class, those who had lived through World War II and its immediate aftermath and who had vivid memories of the time of the action of the novel, would be particularly offended by the novel's portrayal of racism in the West in the forties and fifties. They weren't. One of my students, a woman probably in her middle seventies, claimed that however badly the Nakanes fared in Canada, had they been in Japan as Japanese Cana-dians their treatment would have been worse.

Kogawa, of course, is well aware that xenophobia is not limited to Canada, but her focus is on the particular types — even the minor, homegrown varieties — of racism practised in her country. Thus Naomi appropriately muses on the larger implications of Mr. Barker's small talk. At the same time, Obasan serves this intrusive guest tea, but, while doing so, she remains resolutely herself, free from "the racist's slur" and "the multi-cultural piper's tune," not even in "clamorous" Canada but in some "silent territory" of her own, "defined by her serving hands." There is a certain triumph in that ongoing independent service. She pours his tea but, "unable to see," she "stops half-way before the cup is full" (226), which constitutes another minor victory. Unlike him, she can recognize and accommodate her own failures of vision.

One other crucial event precedes the arrival of Stephen and Aunt Emily and the impending dénouement of the novel. After the Barkers depart, both Obasan and Naomi briefly sleep, and Naomi has another significant dream. It is about "the place of the dead," a broad courtyard where a flower ceremony is underway. The mother, watched by all the other members of the family, is the central participant. "In her mouth she held a knotted string stem" like the twine Obasan saves, and from that stem "hung a rose, red as a heart" (227). But as Naomi moves towards her mother, the dream verges towards nightmare. A Grand Inquisitor figure appears and attempts to pry open both the mother's lips and the daughter's eyes, at which point Naomi awakens to read the dream partly in terms of two ideograms for love. One, the more obvious, is made from the root signs for heart, hand, and action, and thus represents love in its common manifestation as "hands and heart in action together." The other is "formed of 'heart,' 'to tell,' and 'a long thread' " (228). This second character obviously relates to the first part of Naomi's dream of "[t]he dance ceremony of the dead [which] was a slow courtly telling, the heart declaring a long thread knotted to Obasan's twine, knotted to Aunt Emily's package" (228). But even as the mother's telling of her love ties the family (including Obasan and Aunt Emily) together, division and disjunction enter in the form of the Grand Inquisitor who, as a figurative embodiment of Naomi's continuing need to know just how and why she has been deserted, is both a "judgement" of the mother and "a refusal to hear." Moreover, "[t]he more [the Grand Inquisitor] questioned her, the more he was her accuser and murderer. The more he killed her, the deeper her silence became." With "telling" here precluded, the other figure and derivation of love (which is not so different in its root implications from sympathy — that is, the same feeling) comes into play. Sharing the mother's silence and isolation, the daughter no longer asks why she was abandoned. "Did I doubt her love?" Naomi now wonders. "Am I her accuser?" She remembers, too, a poem by the Chinese poet Wu-ti, a kind of working definition of love as both precious and hidden: "*Did you not know that people hide their love / Like a flower that seems too precious to be picked?*" (228).

Naomi sees that the "mother hid her love, but hidden in life... she [might] speak through dream" (228). She has, indeed, just so spoken. "Her tale is a rose with a tangled stem," and even if that tale cannot be fully attended (both the tale and the rose will soon be clearer), "[a]ll this questioning, this clawing at her grave, is an unseemly thing." During "the week of my Uncle's departure," Naomi declares, "let there be peace" (229). That wish will soon be granted. Although she is almost at peace with her memory of the loss of her mother and has almost accepted her absence, she still does not know the answer to the questions she now realizes she should no longer ask. Consistent with the logic of the passage just considered, the answer comes only when she ceases to demand it, and that answer, painful as it is, finally puts her past and her mother to rest.

It is at this point that Stephen and Aunt Emily arrive, accompanied by Nakayama-sensei, who soon picks up the sheets of blue paper Obasan was reading. He first glances at them, and then reads carefully and with evident concentration those "[l]etters from a long time ago." They report something about which he "had no knowledge" (232). Neither, he rightly suspects, do Stephen or Naomi. When this suspicion is confirmed, he claims that, despite the mother's wishes, her two children should know what happened to her, especially since "[t]hey are not children any longer" (232). After Naomi fully concurs with that view, he reads aloud the letters, softly interrupting himself to remind Stephen and Naomi to "[l]isten carefully to [the] voice" that is their "mother ... speaking" (223).[10]

The letters are from Naomi's Grandmother Kato; they are read by Nakayama-sensei; but the story they tell is the mother's. Naomi at last finds out that her mother went in January of 1945 to stay with a cousin in Nagasaki, partly to help with the arrival of the cousin's second child and partly to escape the intensifying bombing of Tokyo. A few months later, and for the same reasons, the grandmother also travelled to Nagasaki. The second baby was a girl who looked almost exactly like Naomi. On the morning of 9 August the second atomic bomb exploded. The two letters in the file date from after this event. The first flatly reports that the grandmother, Naomi's mother, and the baby girl are the only members of the family to have survived. The second is an "outpouring" of the appalling details of their survival (234). They had attempted to let the "horror" die in silence (236), Grandma Kato admits in this second letter, but four years after the bombing it persists and is even growing. As she writes, the baby girl, now four years old, is in a hospital dying of leukemia.

The grandmother's final letter ends with the child's impending death. Sometime later the mother had died too. Her name was found on a list of the dead, Aunt Emily acknowledges, by a missionary who also noted that a Canadian maple tree grew by the plaque that bore her name. There was no memorial other than her earlier directive, contained in the second letter: "Do not tell Stephen and Naomi. . . . I am praying that they may never know" (241). But just as silence did not work for Naomi's mother and her own mother (note the second letter), it did not work for her and Naomi (as the whole novel demonstrates). Naomi, in fact, can now connect her silence regarding the abuse she suffered with her mother's silence after the bomb: "In my dreams, a small child sits with a wound on her knee. The wound on her knee is on the back of her skull, large and moist. A double wound. The child is forever unable to speak. The child forever fears to tell." But "woundedness" was not healed by silence, neither the child's nor the mother's. "Gentle mother," she continues, "we were lost together in our silences. Our wordlessness was our mutual destruction." Now, however, she is "no longer a child [and] can know your presence though you are not here. The letters tonight are skeletons. Bones only. But the earth still stirs with dormant blooms. Love flows through the roots of the trees by our graves" (243). Those last two propositions are proved by Naomi's final action in the novel.

RESOLUTION AND RELEASE

Obasan concludes with another visit to the coulee outside Granton that only partly recapitulates the opening 9 August pilgrimage Naomi made with her uncle. "Nothing changes ne," she had then claimed. A month later much has changed. She goes alone this time, but she is now much more connected to her family and her past. The death of the uncle has precipitated her own reengagement with the previously suppressed memories of her childhood and with the record of the family's past as compiled by Aunt Emily, a personal and a family heritage that Naomi has long declined to review. She now knows, for example, the significance of 9 August as well as the other reasons why her mother never returned. At the end of the novel she can mourn and remember her mother just as, she now knows, her uncle did at the beginning. She can mourn and remember her uncle too. " 'Umi no yo,' he always said. 'It's like the sea' " (247). As her last words in the novel echo his first, past and present, life and death, tragedy and survival seem to merge naturally into one another, and it is somehow appropriate that Uncle is buried beneath the sea of grass that recalls the ocean off British Columbia where he earlier fished in his prized boat and, beyond that, the other side of the same ocean, where his ancestors also sailed. In death, then, Uncle serves as a kind of bridge of dreams to other deaths, and particularly to the death of a Japanese-Canadian woman in Japan.[11] Having come to terms with those deaths, Naomi is, finally, almost at peace with herself. We last see her concerned not with past suffering, but with the present — the flowers bordering the stream that springs up in the ravine: "The perfume in the air is sweet and faint," she notes. "If I hold my head a certain way, I can smell [the flowers] from where I am" (247).

In other ways, too, the conclusion of the novel marks a return to its beginning, but a return with significant differences. The first visit, for example, takes place, we are specifically told, at "9:05 p.m. August 9, 1972" (1), just as night is falling. The second, however, occurs as dawn is beginning to stir. The setting during the first was "so still . . . that if a match were to be lit, the flame would not waiver" (1); but during the second Naomi sees the moon reflected in the rippling stream, "water and stone dancing. . . . a quiet ballet, soundless as breath" (247). As *breath*, not death. And with "Naomi's culminating epiphany . . . the 'stone' of silence and the 'stream' of language" unite, which "brings us full circle [back] to the prose poem that opens the novel" (Goellnicht 297).

That return has already been enacted in the text. When Naomi, at the end of the novel, descends the "steep" walls of the coulee she comes to a physical version of the imagined subterranean stream that has run through the novel and that was particularly posited in the opening poetic epigraph. Words, it will be remembered, were there designated as vain "pock marks on the earth," they were "hailstones seeking an underground stream," a formulation that prompted the speaker (presumably Naomi) to wonder if she "could follow the stream down and down to the hidden voice" and so "come at last to the freeing word?" To this question "the night sky" avouched "no reply." There is no reply at the end of the novel either, but Naomi does go down to the stream and partially enter into it, just as "the underground stream seeps through the earth" to meet her and to coat her shoes with mud. In a way, the question to which the heavens did not respond is here partly answered by the dirt and water, the mud of this earth, and also, of course, by the "perfume . . . sweet and faint" of flowers. "Unless the stone bursts with telling, unless the seed flowers with speech," Naomi had earlier mused, "there is in my life no living word." At the end of the novel the seed flowers, and the blooms evoke both the recent death of her uncle and the earlier death of her mother. Although death precludes their living presence, it does not (especially when that death is, in a merging of ceremony and nature, accepted) preclude their living words, which now must speak in and through Naomi.

" 'Umi no yo,' he always said. 'It's like the sea' " (247). That one-line evocation and summation of Uncle also anticipates and recapitulates the whole novel, which is to say that in still another way the end returns to the beginning. For it is only at the conclusion of *Obasan*, with the second visit to the coulee, that Naomi is ready to go back to the first visit and recount how she comes to the second visit and to a different stance towards silence and speech. She will render the "silence that cannot speak" in the first words of the epigraph into the novel that we have just read. Much like Margaret Laurence's *The Diviners*, but in a rather more subtle fashion, *Obasan* is therefore a circular *Künstlerroman*, the story of how the protagonist/narrator finally became an artist by reaching the point where she could produce the novel we have just read. In that beginning is the novel's end, and in that end is its beginning, and this conjoining of beginning and end particularly fits Naomi's experience as well as its larger context, the experience of Japanese Canadians. Exiled from British Columbia, tragically deprived of their homes, livelihoods, and most of their possessions, these people entered into other lives and other ways of being Japanese and Canadian. The sea of grass could substitute, for example, for the real sea. Silent, sexually victimized as a child and almost autistic as an adult, particularly pained by the prolonged and unexplained absence of her mother, Naomi still must make out of loneliness and loss her life and her story, which is exactly what she finally does as proved by the novel itself.

The novel, however, does not end with the protagonist's final entry into the valley, with the smell of flowers in the early dawn. And appropriately so. As much as some epiphanic acceptance of her own and her family's suffering is necessary for Naomi before she can come to terms with her life (much less come to the telling of that life), it must also be stressed that no possible individual perspective can be adequate to contain the whole tragedy it purports to delimit. Yet *Obasan*, in its last chapter, comes dangerously close to over-resolution, to the implicit assumption that the events of the text have conspired to leave the protagonist standing firm at the end, finally master of those same events she can now narrate. Her mother's death, however, and the belatedly revealed circumstances of that death, can hardly be seen as the price that Naomi has to pay for her own independence, nor did her aunts endure so that she would be spared similar trials. Neither can the gross injustices that Japanese Canadians suffered at the hands of the British Columbia provincial and the Canadian federal governments be turned into some ethnicized little-engine-that-could fable of new beginnings achieved through adversities determinedly overcome. Moreover, as the language of the novel obviously strives, especially at the end of this last chapter, to set up crucially resonant patterns and echoes, it verges toward poetry, but poetry partly in the pejorative sense — as if the very verbal facility whereby Naomi's own story is resolved can somehow outweigh the substance of that story, as if all of that suffering has laboured merely to bring forth, finally, a prose poem.

To avoid just these dangers, the last numbered chapter of the novel, what we might call its first ending, is succeeded by a brief postscript presumably taken from Aunt Emily's voluminous record of governmental action and inaction. This final section and second ending is designated simply: "Excerpt from the memorandum sent by the Co-Operative Committee on Japanese Canadians to the House and the Senate of Canada, April 1946" (248). The "excerpt" reproduced is a three-page, ten-point argument against the government plan, put forth after the war was over, to return all Japanese Canadians to Japan. The presumably Anglo authors of the memorandum argue that these "Orders-in-Council [requiring the deportation of Canadians of Japanese racial origin] are wrong and indefensible" for a number of reasons. They "constitute a violation of International Law"; they "put the value of Canadian citizenship into contempt"; they are "based upon racial discrimination"; they "are in no way related to any war emergency" (nor was there, the writers point out, any real evidence that the emergency of the war required the racist measures earlier enforced); but, chiefly, the proposed orders are themselves "an adoption of the methods of Naziism," and thus "a crime against humanity," much like the offenses for which "the war criminals of Germany and Japan are being tried" (248–50). The last words of this document, and almost the last words of the novel, charging Canada with "the methods of Naziism," reinvoke the whole historic context of the novel, the treatment of Japanese Canadians during and after World War II, and assert that context as enduring beyond and outside any accommodation Naomi comes to with her own past. As various theorists of Holocaust writing have emphasized, the atrocity of Naziism exceeds any possible account of its practice.[12] By concluding the novel with the statement of a public charge, not with an account of a private coming to terms with the consequences of the charged offense, Kogawa makes much the same point. The real issue of the novel, and it is powerfully foregrounded on the last page, is not Naomi's — or the Japanese Canadians' — ability to endure; it is the country's capacity to require such endurance. As certain signs suggest — the military standoff at Oka, the continuing irresolution of Native land claims, politicians and new parties crudely exploiting anti-Québécois feelings after the failure of the Meech Lake Accord — that capacity may well be still too much with us.

In effect, *Obasan* has, I would argue, two open endings. The first, chapter 39, is a Margaret Laurence-style poetic-epiphany resolution that metafictionally returns the novel to its own subject matter and to the problem of turning painful history into artistic narration. The second, the excerpt, is a Margaret Atwood-like power-politics conclusion that not only returns the novel to its own subject matter but also to the different problem of turning painful narration into positive history. The two endings and the two problems are, of course, complementary, which is to say that the art and the politics of a text are always in the service of one another and cannot really be schematically divided in the manner I have just postulated. Indeed, Kogawa employs the two endings to fuse the private and poetic strains in the novel with the public and political ones.

In other ways, too, the two endings are conjoined, starting with the very way in which they differ from one another. As just noted, the second is a kind of corrective to the first, and Naomi's poetic language of final personal transcendence is recontextualized by the stark details and argumentation set forth in the historical document. The document, moreover, addresses the same problem that Naomi has confronted (how to cope with the racial discrimination directed against the Japanese in Canada), and by its public focus calls into question the efficacy of making, as Naomi seems to be doing at the end of chapter 39, one's own separate peace. The double ending of the novel thus effectively recapitulates a feature that runs throughout the whole work — the positioning of the protagonist between her two aunts. Naomi's first, silent coming to terms with things is, after all, a very Obasan-like solution, whereas the articulate public denunciation of the proposed measures of the government as "the methods of Naziism" is precisely what we would expect from Aunt Emily.

This symbolic conjunction of the two aunts at the end of the novel resituates Naomi with respect to each and to the meaning their different experiences have for her. Obasan embodies silence and acquiescence to suffering; despite her long residence in Canada, she lives largely according to traditional Japanese values that emphasize the paramount importance of the family and the community. Personal desires must give way to group needs. Individual expression should be oblique, elusive. In contrast, Aunt Emily, from a Japanese perspective, is hopelessly Westernized, and belligerently assertive. The nail that sticks out, one of the most common of Japanese proverbs proclaims, will be pounded down. Aunt Emily sticks out. She does so, admittedly, as a way of proclaiming her membership in both the Japanese-Canadian community (despite its enforced diaspora) and in the larger community of Canada. Both proclamations are made through a direct and powerful language that articulates a potent dissensus, in short, in a language Obasan would never dream of voicing. Furthermore, and as previously noted, although Naomi long thinks she sides more with Obasan than with Aunt Emily, that preference is not so much her carefully considered position as it is her way of protecting herself from painful knowledge. Indeed, three generations removed from Japan, she can hardly be Japanese in the traditional manner of Obasan but must be, in the mode of Aunt Emily, some combination of Japanese and Canadian. And, by the end of the novel, Naomi has perused much of what she earlier declined to read and has also discovered, especially with respect to the details of the death of her mother, that the burden of past suffering is sometimes made lighter when the suffering is acknowledged. "Gentle Mother," she muses, after she has read the mother's letters, "we were lost together in our silences. Our wordlessness was our mutual destruction" (243). Consequently, as A. Lynne Magnusson suggests, the fact that Naomi puts on Aunt Emily's "warmer" coat as she is leaving for her second and concluding trip to the coulee might well be a sign of her increased acceptance of the pattern represented by Aunt Emily (66). It might also be noted that just as she earlier countered Aunt Emily's ethos by insisting on the futility of words, she also has some later reservations about Obasan's reliance on silence and acceptance. Thus she wonders if it is "enough that Obasan shared her lifetime with Uncle" through all those "long winters in the hut that could not be warmed," and notes that their silent constancy to one another has still led to death and desolation: "Dead hands can no longer touch our outstretched hands or move to heal" (245). In view of these suggestions of a positional shift, it may be that the final section of the novel, the excerpt from Aunt Emily's papers, is put there by Naomi as a last tribute to her Aunt Emily. Certainly this addendum to Naomi's account of how she came to be able to tell her own story places that story in the larger context Aunt Emily always advocated.

Just as the last chapter loops back to the beginning of the book, so does the appended excerpt. The epigraph to the novel begins: "There is a silence that cannot speak. There is a silence that will not speak." One "reply" to the silence here invoked might be articulate argument. Moreover, if the silence of history oppresses, it may well do so because that history itself has been silenced, silenced in Naomi's case by her own reluctance to hear the history that Aunt Emily had to tell. In this sense the "no reply" anticipated at the beginning of the novel has been superseded at the end by three responses: the story of the exile of the mother; the larger story of the family's history as compiled by Aunt Emily; the still larger story of the whole context of that history, including the record of how it was resisted.

As the excerpt shows, the racist policies of the government were resisted, and were resisted by more than just the Aunt Emilys of the Japanese-Canadian community. That crucial fact points to still other social and literary work that reproducing the memorandum (as opposed, say, to quoting from the infamous orders in council themselves) does in *Obasan*. It foregrounds, as noted, the "Naziism" of Canada that needed to be opposed, but foregrounds it in a document demonstrating just such opposition. Furthermore, the precise measures questioned in the excerpt were the only ones, in the whole sorry story of shoddy political leadership and deliberately fanned racism, to be rescinded precisely because the public was effectively persuaded to denounce them as outrageously unjust. Ending by invoking a political and moral argument that worked counters the epigraph's insistence on the futility of language, the "pock mark" theory of words. The second ending thereby emphasizes the political implications of Naomi's personal narrative and allows those implications to extend beyond their immediate import to other analogous situations, whether clearly alluded to in the text (the plight of Native peoples) or not.

The excerpt ending reverberates beyond the text, and it does so more clearly for some readers than for others. In contrast to Ed Kitagawa, Jean Suzuki, and Gordon Nakayama, the three obviously Japanese-Canadian individuals who are named and thanked in the preface, three Anglo names are appended to the "respectfully submitted" postscript document: James M. Finlay, Andrew Brewin, and Hugh MacMillan (250). Although the numerous and not always fully translated and/or annotated Japanese features of the text seem to suggest a book written primarily for a Japanese-Canadian or even Japanese (*Obasan* is popular in Japan) readership, the concluding excerpt compellingly claims an Anglo readership. Of course the book addresses both audiences, but my point is that it is finally and especially directed to readers more likely to see themselves in those who enforced the discrimination than in those who endured it. In effect, the three final Anglo names are a reading directive in the form of a crucial question. Who represents the Anglo-Canadian reader in this text? The three individuals who opposed mass deportation or, say, the custodian of confiscated property, the misnamed functionary, B. Good?

At the end of the novel, a perturbing and powerfully poetic account of one individual's extended confrontation with racism, we are left with the fact of racism in the form of a flat, prosaic argument denouncing one of the more racist measures directed against the Japanese in Canada. Certainly this conjunction of fictional text and historic document invites us to align ourselves with James M. Finlay and company. But the same conjunction also serves to suggest that, although the right inward gestures and recognitions can help to heal lives, they do not necessarily heal history, and that what is true for Naomi as protagonist might be true for us as readers as well. But if her larger commitment to the historical imperative at the end of the text is the metafictional trick of having circled back from that ending to narrate, for our political and moral good, the novel we have just finished, our response to having read it should be something more than sometime going back to the beginning to read it again.

BEYOND AND BACK TO OBASAN

A ready measure of major fiction is how well it repays rereading, and *Obasan*, I have discovered, repays very well. But if the novel moves one to reread it — and to develop a larger concern with the human problems central to it — then a second reading should be informed by more than just the first. Before coming back to Kogawa and her portrayal of the injustices done to Japanese Canadians, the committed reader will want to know more about that whole sad episode in Canada's history. Ken Adachi's *The Enemy That Never Was* is a good place to begin, as is Ann Gomer Sunahara's *The Politics of Racism: The Uprooting of Japanese Canadians during the Second World War*. A larger context for these two studies can be found in Patricia E. Roy's *A White Man's Province: British Columbia Politicians and Chinese and Japanese Immigrants, 1858–1914*, as well as Ronald Takaki's *Strangers from a Different Shore: A History of Asian Americans*, which describes the reception in America of every group of Asian immigrants and also takes the subtitle of its first chapter, "From a Different Shore: Their History Bursts with Telling," from "Joy Kogawa's wonderful phrase" (9). I would also recommend John Herd Thompson's *Ethnic Minorities during Two World Wars*. As Thompson points out, the concentration camps of World War I anticipated the "Japanese" policy of World War II, despite the obvious senselessness of that first exercise in racist wartime patriotism, seen, for example, in such episodes as Ukrainians who wished to enlist in the Canadian armed forces being caught in the catch-22 of having to lie about, or confess to, their ethnic origin, when either alternative could land them in an internment camp instead of in the army. Canada's "physical treatment of those defined as internal enemies," Thompson concludes, was worse than the United States's or Great Britain's, better than Germany's or Japan's, "but a parliamentary democracy can hardly take refuge behind the argument that its mistreatment of minorities was less ruthless than that of Nazi Germany or Imperial Japan" (17). Roger Daniels makes a fuller comparison of what happened in Canada and in the United States in his *Concentration Camps: North American Japanese in the United States and Canada during World War II*, while, more recently, two Canadian historians, Patricia E. Roy and J.L. Granatstein, and two Japanese historians, Masako Iino and Hiroko Takamura, in *Mutual Hostages: Canadians and Japanese during the Second World War*, comparatively assess each country's treatment of internees from the other. (Granatstein has also recently argued — quite unconvincingly, I think — that Canada's wartime treatment of Japanese Canadians was fully justified.)

Still other texts and perspectives besides the academic and the historical can be brought to bear on *Obasan*. In *Years of Sorrow, Years of Shame: The Story of the Japanese Canadians in World War II*, Barry Broadfoot weaves together the anonymous testimony of many "survivors," both Caucasian and Japanese Canadian, to give a composite oral history of the time, which is, in its way, almost as powerful as *Obasan*. Consider Broadfoot's last entry, titled "It Could Happen Again":

You ask if it could happen again?
I'd like to say no but I don't believe it. I don't think human nature changes that much. There is still hysteria, still racial prejudice, still economic pressure, and I would say that today we have more selfishness than we've ever had in our past history, individual as well as collective selfishness. (370)

Fifteen years later, after the "me" decade (the 1980s) and the recent wave of "Japan bashing" in the United States, these words seem rather more ominous than they did in 1977. Broadfoot's sources may be too undifferentiated in their anonymity, but this problem is countered in Keibo Oiwa's *Stone Voices: Wartime Writings of Japanese Canadian Issei*, which, as Kogawa herself notes in the foreword, serves to show the "mix of shadings and colours" of the Japanese-

Canadian contribution to the "patchwork quilt" of Canada (6). There are also moving individual accounts of Japanese-Canadian wartime experience such as Shizuye Takashima's *A Child in Prison Camp* or Muriel Kitagawa's *This Is My Own* (a collection of letters edited by Roy Miki). Kitagawa's letters are particularly relevant because they partly prompted Kogawa to write *Obasan* when she came across them in the Public Archives in Ottawa, and because Kitagawa is the model for Aunt Emily in the novel. Fortunately, we need no longer search the archives for such counterhistory, for the victims' view of what their oppression was and meant.

Kogawa's other writing can also help to illuminate the art of *Obasan*. As Coral Ann Howells points out, "Joy Kogawa is a poet who ... is acutely aware of the multiple possibilities within language, of its power to distort and lie which is matched only by its power to create texts of subtly interwoven images which shadow the life of the psyche." Out of this honed awareness, Kogawa writes "an intricately structured [novel] of interconnecting threads binding together the present and the past, the living and the dead by feeling, intuition and dream" (125–26). The very foregrounding of that final "dream" is anticipated, of course, by the title and the poems of the early volume *A Choice of Dreams* (1974), and the same title and poems also situate the writer and the writing somewhere between a dream of Canada and a dream of Japan. But then, as Kogawa has observed elsewhere, "a Canadian is a hyphen and ... we're diplomats by birth" ("Interview" 96). As both *A Choice of Dreams* and *Obasan* attest, part of a Canadian writer's inherited task is the continuous writing and unwriting of that conjoining and dividing hyphen.

Individual poems also help to clarify the dense symbolism employed in *Obasan* and serve to throw into clearer relief crucial details of the novel. Thus, in "Public Bath," a poem about the Japanese *ofuro* in which everyone steams into one "warm soft body blending," the poet wonders:

> Would that this could be exported home
> And politicians and business men and sons
> Could meet together in the public bath
> To batter and scrub each other raw
> And dissolve the ills of the day (*Choice* 22)

Of course the *ofuro* was exported to Canada, but no multicultural bathing took place in British Columbia before or during the Second World War. Still, this poem suggests why, in Slocan, the Japanese Canadians cleaved to the tradition of the communal bath and hints that Canada might well have borrowed, literally and figuratively, this custom.

The cry of the bantam rooster, which sounds so ominously in *Obasan* (the sky *is* falling!), is given, however, a different subtext in "Rooster" when that poem concludes:

> With the rooster calling
> His feet rooted in the night
> His wings in the morning this is
> Still the time
> To forgive, to be forgiven (*Choice* 86)

The biblical implications of this calling counter the Chicken Little ones in *Obasan*, especially when the rooster crows three times — and the "neighbour's dog [similarly] barks three short excited blasts" (170). Above the denial of the falling sky, the heavens still hang firm. And below some things do, too, as is suggested by the beautifully muted "communion" scene that ends this chapter: "Obasan turns down the coal-oil lamp and, cupping her hand behind the chimney, she blows out the night's light. She hands us all pieces of toast" (171).

As even their titles suggest, many of Kogawa's other poems — "The Chicken Killing" and "Trunk in the Attic" from *A Choice of Dreams*, "Bread to Stone" and "Like Spearing a Butterfly" from *Jericho Road* — also relate to *Obasan*. But the one Kogawa work that most clearly supplements the first novel is the second, the recently published *Itsuka* (1992). This sequel shows that there is, for Naomi, life after *Obasan*, a proposition only faintly anticipated in that first novel's conclusion by the smell of wild roses that comes to the protagonist as she stands again in the same coulee she and her uncle visited in the opening episode. Although she finally knows the fuller story of her life of loneliness and loss, that knowledge constitutes the grounds for revisioning a past, not for claiming a future. Indeed, as Naomi looks back to the immediately preceding death of her uncle and beyond that to the death of her mother on the other side of a sea that is itself lost to her and her family, it is hard to see any let-us-then-be-up-and-doing affirmation in her epiphanic retrospection. Moreover, the only clear promise for the future at the end of *Obasan* is the impending demise of Obasan, who is last seen silently praying over Uncle's wartime identification card and who will soon follow him into death as she earlier followed him into exile. Since Naomi's main relationships were with Uncle and Obasan, not Aunt Emily or Stephen, what awaits her after the deaths of these two ties to life? The answer *Itsuka* provides is surprising. Toronto. Love. Political involvement.

Briefly, *Itsuka* records how, after the lingering death of Obasan, Aunt Emily insists, quite rightly, that Naomi now has no real reason for remaining in Alberta, and sweeps her niece along with her when she returns to Toronto. Slowly establishing herself in that city, Naomi begins to work for a multicultural magazine significantly named *Bridge*, and tentatively embarks on a romantic relationship with her employer, Father Cedric, an eccentric Anglican priest who particularly appreciates Naomi's reticence (she reminds him of his half-Métis mother). Largely because of Father Cedric's interest, Naomi finds herself engaged in, if not committed to, the Japanese-Canadian movement for apology and redress. But as she watches others try to claim and contain this cause, she becomes more involved, more her Aunt Emily's advocate and ally, and the novel concludes with the government, after many fits and starts, offering a real apology and substantial financial compensation instead of a token acknowledgement that some injustice probably occurred.

As even this cursory summary indicates, *Itsuka* continues the story told in *Obasan* in two crucial respects, and Kogawa emphasizes the importance of that double continuation by reemploying as an epigraph to the second novel one of the epigraphs of the first, the brief biblical promise of a "new name written" in the proffered stone. At the end of *Obasan*, Naomi has broken through the stone silence that has long surrounded her, but that break has not produced a new Naomi. She also has to break through the stone self she has constructed to protect herself from too much pain — a personal transformation largely achieved in *Itsuka*. Moreover, her private double reassertion of story and identity is then reenacted on a larger, public level. As a case study of, on the one hand, the politics of protest and, on the other, the contradictions of a sham multiculturalism, the novel traces how the Japanese-Canadian community reestablished itself by insisting on its own version of its own history and its own agenda for redress.

Again, story, voice, and identity are central, interrelated issues. Official Canada, personified in the novel by Dr. Clive Stinson, "vice-president of St. John's College [which publishes *Bridge* magazine], fellow of the Royal Military Academy and consultant to Ottawa's Multicultural Directorate" (149), claims that some acknowledgement of the injustice done to Japanese Canadians might be in order, yet blandly dismisses as "rabble rousing" and "personal bias" any account of the unfortunate episode that differs from the one he would prefer to believe (150, 152). In this duplicitous enterprise he and his ilk are, unfortunately, abetted by a few Japanese Canadians who seek status and recognition through telling those in power precisely what they want to hear. For example, Nikki Kagami even assures Stinson that, had Canada been invaded by Japan, the "majority" of Japanese Canadians would have been "loyal to the enemy" (230), so he need not even believe in the "injustice" he will only partially admit existed. Small wonder Stinson finds Nikki Kagami "an appropriate spokesperson" for her people (150), and praises her "co-operative attitude" (225) as a form of higher patriotism quite lacking in the leaders of the National Japanese Canadian League who are, he maintains, demanding financial reimbursement only to enrich themselves.

The "truth," Stinson occasionally acknowledges, "is a matter of perspective" (225), yet the only perspective that matters to him is his own. For such a man, and for officially multicultural Canada (Stinson is, after all, a "consultant" to the wonderfully misnamed "Multicultural Directorate"), multiculturalism is, in Janice Kulyk Keefer's apt phrasing, a policy of encouraging "ethnic and racial minorities to stick to singing 'pretty songs' instead of allowing them 'access to power'" (35). By organizing to confront a definition of who and what they should be as "victims" that is almost as skewed as the earlier definition of who they were as "traitors," Japanese Canadians begin to come into themselves individually and collectively. As Naomi at one point poetically puts it, "within our cocoons, something is being formed. One by one, we are coming forth with dewy fresh wings. The more meetings we attend, the more we need to attend. We're learning how to fly by stuffing envelopes" (211). The measure of the success of that collective transformation is provided by the afterword, an official pronouncement that parallels the political postscript to *Obasan*, the demand that the "methods of Naziism" be resisted (250). So, too, must the method of a monologic multiculturalism. At the end of *Itsuka* the Japanese-Canadian community has reestablished itself by gaining, as the prime minister's "Acknowledgement" attests, the redress that it wanted, and not the token apology Nikki Kagami advocated in the name of the community she thereby denied.

From biblical epigraph to official afterword, *Itsuka* effectively redeploys the structure of *Obasan* even as it carries the story told in that first novel forward to the crucial event of the Canadian government officially admitting the wrongness of the policies it formulated to dispossess Japanese Canadians and then send them into internal exile. The two novels thus constitute a larger and more public loop in time than that enacted in *Obasan*, and, indeed, Naomi, at the end of *Itsuka*, retrospectively reinvokes the retrospective ending of the earlier novel. Standing with Cedric above the Ottawa River on a hill "not unlike the slope to the Old Man River near Granton," she recalls how she stood with her uncle 16 years previously, and, "in the coolness of a night like this, looking down at the ocean of grass," heard him say, "as he always did, 'Umi no yo.' It's like the sea." She remembers also something else he sometimes said: "There is a time for crying. . . . But itsuka, someday, the time for laughter will come." For her, that time has come, and as "telling leaps over the barricades and the dream enters day" (288), the past merging of prairie and sea, of life and death, of tragic loss and promise in the scent of roses is itself merged into another evocation of the multiplicity of human and transcendent existence:

I can hear the waves from childhood rippling outwards to touch other children who wait for their lives. I can hear the voices, faint as the far-away sound of a distant, almost inaudible wind. It's the sound of the underground stream. It speaks through memory, through dream, through our hands, through our words, our arms, our trusting. I can hear the sound of the voice that frees, a light, steady, endless breath. I can hear the breath of life. (288)

Not everything, however, is wrapped up with *Itsuka*'s concluding "itsuka." The relationship between Naomi and Father Cedric still seems as tenuous as ever. Naomi and Stephen are now even more sundered than they were at the conclusion of *Obasan*, so much so that "Naomi's involvement with Father Cedric seems," as Keefer maintains, "a rather unconvincing substitute for what might have been the heart of the novel — the failure of Naomi's relationship with her brother Stephen, and the crucial questions raised by his abdication from any involvement with family or community..." (35). As Naomi herself, near the end, admits:

It would take a miracle, I think, to bridge the distance between us now. It's as impossible for me to reach him as it is for . . . the entire Japanese Canadian community to reach Government. Still — who knows? Maybe someday — itsuka, itsuka, perhaps — via music, via letter. (270–71)

But the consideration that the Japanese-Canadian community does finally reach the government suggests that there may be still another "itsuka" beyond the at last realized "some time" with which this novel concludes. If this is so, neither Kogawa as author nor we as readers are yet done with Naomi Nakane and her ongoing story.

NOTES

1 Good theoretical discussions of colonialism and representation can be found in Homi K. Bhabha's *Nation and Narration* and Abdul R. JanMohamed's *Manichean Aesthetics*, or, for more specifically Canadian reference, Bill Ashcroft, Gareth Griffiths, and Helen Tiffin's *The Empire Writes Back* and Ian Adam and Helen Tiffin's *Past the Last Post*.

2 Numerous entries in Libby Scheier, Sarah Sheard, and Eleanor Wachtel's *Language in Her Eye* address this question and, taken together, constitute one of the better discussions of the whole difficult matter.

3 Kogawa herself has commented that she "still think[s] that the people who have [her] parents [sic] house have stolen property" (qtd. in Fujita 41n3).

4 The larger story has perhaps begun to be told, however, in such collections as Shirley Neuman and Smaro Kamboureli's *A Mazing Space*, Barbara Godard's *Gynocritics/Gynocritiques*, and Sky Lee's (and others') *Telling It*. However, as Kogawa has observed of her own Japanese-Canadian experience, each "situation is unique" and "should be addressed on its own terms" (Corbeil 1), so no composite story can replace all the particular, individual ones.

5 Patricia E. Roy, in *A White Man's Province*, details the development of anti-Oriental prejudice in British Columbia, while W. Peter Ward, in "British Columbia and the Japanese Evacuation," gives a good, brief historical account of how that prejudice was put into action after the Japanese attack on Pearl Harbor and Canada's entry into a war against Japan.

6 See also Henderson for an excellently annotated, slightly different translation of the poem (27).

7 In much the same vein, the expulsion was, from the first, euphemistically termed an "evacuation," which, "in ordinary usage, is something that is done for the benefit of those evacuated," and thus the very "opposite" of "[w]hat happened to the Japanese Canadians" (Cohn 3n2).

8 Momotaro is also silent for many years, and this "parallels" Naomi's long silence before telling her story (Fairbanks 90).

9 Kaoru Ikeda, for example, in her "Slocan Diary," records finding "several precious *matsutake* mushrooms" and enjoying "our first dish [of *matsutake* rice] in many years" (149).

10 The fact that the absent mother here speaks through the voice of a clergyman father figure who has the name and occupation of Kogawa's own father raises, as Magdalene Redekop notes in her interview with the author, an important question about the congruence of "the voices of the spiritual fathers" as compared to those "of the 'real mothers'" (Kogawa, "Literary Politics" 17).

11 Goody points out that Kogawa, throughout the novel, conjoins bridge and dream to echo and ironically reverse Junichiro Tanizaki's *The Bridge of Dreams* as well as the chapter of the same name that concludes Lady Murasaki Shikibu's *The Tale of Genji* (158–60).

12 As Elie Wiesel has asserted: "He or she who did not live through the event will never know it. And he or she who did live through the event will never reveal it. Not entirely. Not really" (7). More recently, David Patterson, in *The Shriek of Silence*, makes, as even his title suggests, much the same point: "words invariably betray silence," and especially the silence of the Holocaust (83).

Works Cited

Adachi Ken. *The Enemy That Never Was: A History of the Japanese Canadians.* Toronto: McClelland, 1976.

Adam, Ian, and Helen Tiffin, eds. *Past the Last Post: Theorizing Post-Colonialism and Post-Modernism.* Calgary: U of Calgary P, 1990.

Ashcroft, Bill, Gareth Griffiths, and Helen Tiffin. *The Empire Writes Back: Theory and Practice in Post-Colonial Literature.* New Accents. London: Routledge, 1989.

Basho, Matsuo. "The Narrow Road of Oku." Trans. Donald Keene. *Anthology of Japanese Literature: From the Earliest Era to the Mid-Nineteenth Century.* Ed. Donald Keene. UNESCO Collection of Representative Works, Japanese Series. New York: Grove, 1955. 363–73.

Bhabha, Homi K., ed. *Nation and Narration.* London: Routledge, 1990.

Blodgett, E.D. *Configurations: Essays on the Canadian Literatures.* Downsview, ON: ECW, 1982.

Broadfoot, Barry. *Years of Sorrow, Years of Shame: The Story of the Japanese Canadians in World War II.* Toronto: Doubleday, 1977.

Cohn, Werner. "The Persecution of Japanese Canadians and the Political Left in British Columbia, December 1941–March 1942." *bc Studies* 68 (1985–86): 3–22.

Collins, Anne. "A White and Deadly Silence." Rev. of *Obasan. Maclean's* 13 July 1981: 54.

Corbeil, Carol. "Kogawa: A Tale of Two Worlds." *Globe and Mail* 14 May 1983: E1.
    A wide-ranging, informative interview.

Daniels, Roger. *Concentration Camps, North America: Japanese in the United States and Canada during World War II.* Malabar, FL: Krieger, 1981.

Douglas, Mary. *Purity and Danger: An Analysis of Concepts of Pollution and Taboo.* New York: Praeger, 1966.

Fairbanks, Carol. "Joy Kogawa's *Obasan*: A Study in Political Efficacy." *Journal of American and Canadian Studies* [Japan] 5 (1990): 73–92.
    A basic assessment of the novel intended for Japanese readers and employing some concepts, such as "*giri,* duty to one's group and country" (81), that do not really translate into English.

French, William. Rev. of *Obasan*. *Globe and Mail* 20 June 1981: E15.

Fujita, Gayle K. " 'To Attend the Sound of Stone': The Sensibility of Silence in *Obasan*." *Melus* 12.3 (1985): 33–42.

Emphasizes the importance of "ethnic heritage as a source of self-realization" (34), and explores Naomi Nakane's *nikkei* (of Japanese ancestry) identity.

Godard, Barbara, ed. *Gynocritics/Gynocritiques: Feminist Approaches to Canadian and Quebec Women's Writing*. Toronto: ECW, 1987.

Goellnicht, Donald C. "Minority History as Metafiction: Joy Kogawa's *Obasan*." *Tulsa Studies in Women's Literature* 8 (1989): 287–306.

Assesses the novel as a historiographic metafiction.

Goody, Ila. "The Stone Goddess and the Frozen Mother: Accomplices of Desire and Death in Tanizaki, *Tay John*, and *Obasan*." *Nature and Identity in Canadian and Japanese Literature*. Publications Series 4.1. Ed. Kinya Tsuruta and Theodore Goossen. Toronto: University of Toronto and York University Joint Centre for Asia Pacific Studies, 1988. 143–66.

Situates *Obasan* between Japanese and English-Canadian literary paradigms.

Gottlieb, Erika. "The Riddle of Concentric Worlds in 'Obasan.' " *Canadian Literature* 109 (1986): 34–53.

A poetic reading of the structure of the novel providing good insights into the significance of Naomi's dreams.

Granatstein, J.L. "A Realist Critique of the Received Version: The Evacuation of the Japanese-Canadians, 1942." *On Guard for Thee: War, Ethnicity, and the Canadian State, 1939–1945*. Ed. Norman Hillmer, Bohdan Kordan, and Lubomyr Luciuck. Ottawa: Canadian Committee for the History of the Second World War, 1988.

Harris, Mason. "Broken Generations in 'Obasan': Inner Conflict and the Destruction of Community." *Canadian Literature* 127 (1990): 41–57.

Interprets Naomi in terms of problematically different (*Issei, Nisei, Sansei*) patterns of assimilation.

Henderson, Harold G., ed. *An Introduction to Haiku: An Anthology of Poems and Poets from Basho to Shiki*. Garden City, NY: Doubleday, 1958.

Howells, Coral Ann. *Private and Fictional Words: Canadian Women Novelists of the 1970s and 1980s*. London: Methuen, 1987.

A sensitive discussion of *Obasan* (118–29) is effectively placed in the larger context of contemporary Canadian women's writing.

Hutcheon, Linda. *The Canadian Postmodern: A Study of Contemporary English-Canadian Fiction*. Toronto: Oxford UP, 1988.

Ikeda, Kaoru. "Slocan Diary." Oiwa 115–54.

Itwaru, Arnold Harrichand. *The Invention of Canada: Literary Text and the Immigrant Imaginary*. Toronto: TSAR, 1990.

JanMohamed, Abdul R. *Manichean Aesthetics: The Politics of Literature in Colonial Africa*. Amherst: U of Massachusetts P, 1983.

Jones, Manina. "The Avenues of Speech and Silence: Telling Difference in Joy Kogawa's *Obasan.*" *Theory between the Disciplines: Authority/Vision/Politics.* Ed. Martin Kreiswirth and Mark A. Cheetham. Ann Arbor: U of Michigan P, 1990. 213–29.

Some astute observations make one wish for still more matter and fewer dropped names.

Keefer, Janice Kulyk. "A Celebration of Difference." Rev. of *Itsuka. Books in Canada* Apr. 1992: 35.

Kilgore, Kathryn. "A Long Way from Home." Rev. of *Obasan. Village Voice* 22 June 1982: 45.

Kitagawa, Muriel. *This Is My Own: Letters to Wes and Other Writings on Japanese Canadians, 1941–1948.* Ed. Roy Miki. Vancouver: Talonbooks, 1985.

Kogawa, Joy. *A Choice of Dreams.* Toronto: McClelland, 1974.

———. Foreword. Oiwa 6.

———. "Interview by Magdalene Redekop." *Other Solitudes: Canadian Multicultural Fictions.* Ed. Linda Hutcheon and Marion Richmond. Toronto: Oxford UP, 1990. 94–101.

———. *Itsuka.* Toronto: Viking, 1992.

———. *Jericho Road.* Toronto: McClelland, 1977.

———. "The Literary Politics of the Victim." With Magdalene Redekop. *Canadian Forum* Nov. 1989: 14–17.

A comparison of *Obasan* with the sequel Kogawa was writing conducted through an interview with the author.

———. *Obasan.* 1981. Markham, ON: Penguin, 1983.

"Kogawa, Joy." *Canada's Who's Who.* Ed. Kieran Simpson. 1991 ed.

Lee, Sky, et al., eds. *Telling It: Women and Language across Cultures, the transformation of a conference.* Vancouver: Press Gang, 1990.

Lim, Shirley Geok-Lin. "Japanese American Women's Life Stories: Maternality in Monica Sone's *Nisei Daughter* and Joy Kogawa's *Obasan.*" *Feminist Studies* 16 (1990): 289–312.

The essay, like its title, too often ignores the fact that Naomi Nakane is Japanese Canadian, and the mostly summary comparison is excessively theoretical.

Magnusson, A. Lynn. "Language and Longing in Joy Kogawa's 'Obasan.'" *Canadian Literature* 116 (1988): 58–66.

An excellent study of the novel that focuses on the Japanese and Lacanian implications of "Kogawa's pervasive concern with the act of speech itself" (58).

Martin, Sandra. "The Haunting of the Japanese." Rev. of *Obasan. Globe and Mail* 10 Apr. 1982: E16.

Merivale, P. "Framed Voice: The Polyphonic Elegies of Hébert and Kogawa." *Canadian Literature* 116 (1988): 68–82.

This perceptive comparison of *Obasan* and Anne Hébert's *Les fous de Bassan* aptly demonstrates the Canadian proclivity for, in Robert Kroetsch's phrase, "dreams of origin."

Milton, Edith. "Unnecessary Precautions." Rev. of *Obasan*. *New York Times Book Review* 5 Sept. 1982: 8, 17.

Moss, John. "Joy Kogawa." *A Reader's Guide to the Canadian Novel.* 2nd ed. Toronto: McClelland, 1987. 201–03.

Neuman, Shirley, and Smaro Kamboureli, eds. *A Mazing Space: Writing Canadian Women Writing.* Edmonton. Longspoon-NeWest, 1986.

"Ode to Joy." *Books in Canada* Apr. 1982: 4–5.

Oiwa, Keibo, ed. *Stone Voices: Wartime Writings of Japanese Canadian Issei.* Trans. Oiwa. Montreal: Véhicule, 1991.

Patterson, David. *The Shriek of Silence: A Phenomenology of the Holocaust Novel.* Lexington: UP of Kentucky, 1992.

Rose, Marilyn Russell. "Hawthorne's 'Custom House,' Said's *Orientalism* and Kogawa's *Obasan*: An Intertextual Reading of an Historical Fiction." *Dalhousie Review* 67 (1987): 286–96.

Reads the novel as an "endorsement of history" that "attacks a central and ingrained Japanese-Canadian value, silence" (295).

————. "Politics into Art: Kogawa's *Obasan* and the Rhetoric of Fiction." *Mosaic* 21 (1988): 215–26.

Assesses the novel's passionate fictionalizing of history and also counters J.L. Granatstein's claim "that the internment of Japanese-Canadians was entirely justifiable" (Rose, "Politics" 225).

Roy, Patricia E. *A White Man's Province: British Columbia Politicians and Chinese and Japanese Immigrants, 1858–1914.* Vancouver: U of British Columbia P, 1989.

Roy, Patricia E., et al. *Mutual Hostages: Canadians and Japanese during the Second World War.* Toronto: U of Toronto P, 1990.

Scheier, Libby, Sarah Sheard, and Eleanor Wachtel, eds. *Language in Her Eye: Views on Writing and Gender by Canadian Women Writing in English.* Toronto: Coach House, 1990.

Sollors, Werner. *Beyond Ethnicity: Consent and Descent in American Culture.* New York: Oxford UP, 1986.

St. Andrews, B.A. "Reclaiming a Canadian Heritage: Kogawa's *Obasan*." *International Fiction Review* 13 (1986): 29–31.

A brief summary review.

Sunahara, Ann Gomer. *The Politics of Racism: The Uprooting of Japanese Canadians during the Second World War.* Toronto: Lorimer, 1981.

Takaki, Ronald. *Strangers from a Different Shore: A History of Asian Americans.* 1989. New York: Viking-Penguin, 1990.

Takashima, Shizuye. *A Child in Prison Camp.* Montreal: Tundra, 1971.

Thomas, Hilda L. "A Time to Remember." Rev. of *Obasan*, by Joy Kogawa;

and *The Politics of Racism*, by Ann Gomer Sunahara. *Canadian Literature* 96 (1983): 103–05.

Thompson, John Herd. *Ethnic Minorities during Two World Wars.* Canada's Ethnic Groups 19. Ottawa: Canadian Historical Association, 1991.

Tsutsumi, Toshiko. "Japanese-Canadian Literature in the Multicultural Society." *Report on Canadian Studies* [Japan] 4 (1983): 107–09.
  Sees *Obasan* as encouraging a rapprochement between *Issei* and *Nisei.*

Ward, W. Peter. "British Columbia and the Japanese Evacuation." *After Confederation.* Toronto: Oxford UP, 1986. 315–32. Vol. 2 of *Interpreting Canada's Past.* Ed. J.M. Bumsted. 2 vols. 1986.

Wayne, Joyce. "Joy Kogawa and the Language of Silence." Rev. of *Obasan. Quill and Quire* Apr. 1981: 34.
  Contains a brief interview with Kogawa.

We Japanese: Being Descriptions of Many of the Customs, Manners, Ceremonies, Festivals, Arts and Crafts of the Japanese besides Numerous Other Subjects. 1934. Miyanoshita: Fujiya Hotel, 1950.

Wiesel, Elie. "The Holocaust as Literary Inspiration." *Dimensions of the Holocaust: Lectures at Northwestern University.* Elie Wiesel, et al. Evanston: Northwestern U, 1977. 5–19.

Willis, Gary. "Speaking the Silence: Joy Kogawa's *Obasan.*" *Studies in Canadian Literature* 12 (1987) 239–50.
  A broadly humanist reading of the novel.

Index

Nakane, Grandma (character) 55, 56
Nakane, Grandpa (character) 33,
   35, 46, 67
Nakayama, Gordon 25, 81
Nakayama-sensei (character) 56, 73
Naomi (character) 15, 16, 20, 21, 24,
   25, 29–89 passim
Naomi's Road (Kogawa) 11
Nomura-obasan (character) 57–58

Obasan (character) 18, 21, 27, 29,
   31, 32, 34–38, 40, 48, 50–55, 57,
   61, 63, 65, 66, 69, 70–72, 79–80, 86
Oiwa, Keibo 83
Old Man Gower (character) 42–46,
   61

Ricci, Nino 16
Rose, Marilyn Russell 19
Rough Lock Bill (character) 58–61
Roy, Patricia E. 82, 83

St. Andrews, B.A. 19
Sam (character) 21
Sollors, Werner 22
Splintered Moon, The (Kogawa) 10
Stephen (character) 33, 47–49, 54,
   56–58, 62–64, 66, 68–70, 72–74,
   86, 89
Sunahara, Ann Gomer 18, 82
Suzuki, Jean 81
Suzuki, T. Buck 25

Takaki, Ronald 82
Takamura, Hiroko 83
Takashima, Shizuye 84
Thomas, Hilda L. 18
Thompson, John Herd 13, 82–83
Tucker, Grace 25

Uncle (character) 30–34, 37, 47, 49,
   53, 56–57, 65, 66, 70, 73, 75, 76,
   80, 86

Wang Wei 50
Wayne, Joyce 17

Willis, Gary 19, 21
Woman in the Woods (Kogawa) 11
Wu Ti 72

Writing against the silence : Joy
Kogawa's Obasan / Arnold Davidson.
Main circ stacks

Bib Id: 16478
813.54 DAV

Important: Do not remove this
date due reminder.

DATE DUE

NOV 1 8 '97